ARB (PHOTOS, ESSAYS, CATALOG)

Entwickelt und entworfen von
Developed and designed by
Franziska Schott & Marco Schibig

ARB
(PHOTOS,
ESSAYS,
CATALOG)

Mit Beiträgen von / With contributions by
Lore Ditzen, Peter Grueneisen, Thomas Keller,
Benedikt Loderer, Peter Lüem, Dominique Uldry e.a.

BIRKHÄUSER – PUBLISHERS FOR ARCHITECTURE
BASEL · BOSTON · BERLIN

"He's so consistently inconsistent."

Andrew Nathaniel White III
on John Coltrane

DER UMFASSENDE ANSATZ ÜBER- WINDET DAS DOGMA

Peter Grueneisen, Los Angeles

THE INCLUSIVE APPROACH BYPASSES DOGMA

Attribute wie detailorientiert, präzise, reduktionistisch, technisch hervorragend, konstruktiv sauber, einfach, traditionell modern sind häufig in Diskussionen über schweizerische und im speziellen bernische Architekturbüros. In einer kritisch gestimmten Runde könnten sogar Begriffe wie pedantisch, dogmatisch, banal oder engstirnig aufkommen.

Discussions about Swiss, or in particular Bernese architectural firms, will often yield attributes such as precise, detail-oriented, reductionist, technically superior, constructively clean, simple or traditionally modern. Even descriptions like pedantic, dogmatic, simplistic or narrow-minded could come up, if the participants are in a more critical mood.

Selten werden Architekten aus dieser Region bezichtigt, allzu kosmopolitisch, zu erfinderisch oder generell zu wild und freizügig zu sein. In dieser Stadt mit einer aussergewöhnlichen Dichte an Architekten bewegen sich die gebauten Resultate, trotz grosser Konkurrenz, meist innerhalb eines ziemlich voraussehbaren Spektrums. Traditionelle Methoden haben einen hohen Stellenwert, philosophisch, konstruktiv, architektonisch und in der Organisation der Büros.

Während diese Tugenden arb keineswegs fremd sind, enthüllt die nähere Betrachtung stille Überraschungen. Still, weil trotz der meist durchgehend hohen Qualität die Arbeiten kaum bekannt sind. Und überraschend wegen der allumfassenden und weitgefächerten Interessen und Methoden, die das Büro im praktischen Verhalten und im Entwurf anwendet.

Rückblickend ist es also nicht verwunderlich, dass ich 1983, frisch aus der Schule, zwar noch nie etwas von arb gehört hatte, jedoch durch den Pianisten und Jazz-Journalisten Franz Biffiger darauf stiess. Er war nicht nur Mentor der

Rarely are architects from that region accused of being too cosmopolitan, too daring, too inventive, or generally too free-spirited. In a place that has one of the densest populations of architects per capita anywhere, the built results mostly fall into a fairly predictable range, despite fierce competition. Traditional methods are highly valued, philosophically, constructively, architecturally, and in the way architects organize their firms. While adhering to many of the principles mentioned above, the firm of arb can be seen as a quiet surprise in this context. Quiet because there is not much publicity surrounding the work, even though most of it is of a very high overall quality. And a surprise because of the inclusive and widespread interests and working methods employed in the firm's approach to practice and design.

In hindsight, it is not surprising that, fresh out of school in 1983, one wasn't really familiar with arb but would be introduced to the pianist and jazz journalist Franz Biffiger. He was not only a mentor of the jazz music scene and of many

7

Jazz-Szene und vieler internationaler Musiker, sondern selbst ein hochbegabter Pianist, sozialdemokratischer Grossrat im Kantonsparlament, Oberst der Milizarmee und last but not least einer der Partner bei arb.

Kurt Aellens langjährige Tätigkeit als Professor in Lausanne und Genf und seine zahlreichen Verbindungen mit Frankreich und dem französischsprachigen Teil der Schweiz sind ebenso Teil der Firmenphilosophie. Die Zusammenarbeit mit Jean Prouvé und anderen französischen Architekten, Künstlern und Ingenieuren formt das

Ulmizberg

Büro und erweitert es weit über die Berner Grenzen hinaus, geographisch wie philosophisch. Als gegenwärtiger Präsident des Schweizerischen Ingenieur- und Architekten-Vereins (SIA) könnte sich Aellens Beitrag auf landesweiter Ebene als äusserst notwendige Öffnung des Berufs in verschiedenen Bereichen erweisen.

Ähnlich weitgefächerte und scheinbar widersprüchliche Interessen und Leistungen sind den weiteren Partnern und vielen Mitarbeitern gemeinsam und tragen zum eklektischen und manchmal chaotischen Arbeitsstil bei, der ganz deutlich die gebaute Arbeit beeinflusst.

Das Engagement in Kunst und multikulturellen Verbindungen wird mit Thomas Kellers und Peter Kellers Forschungsar-

international musicians but himself an accomplished player, held public office as a social democrat in the state parliament, was a high ranking officer in the Swiss militia army and, of course, was one of the partners at arb.

Kurt Aellen's long-standing activity as an educator in Lausanne and Geneva, his close connections with France and the French part of Switzerland are defining traits in the firm's philosophy. Collaborations with Jean Prouvé and other French architects, artists and engineers shape the firms outlook and expand it far beyond the borders, both geographically and philosophically. As the current president of the SIA, his contributions on a national level may prove to be a highly needed opening of the profession in many areas.

Similarly broad and sometimes seemingly conflicting interests and accomplishments are common for all four of the partners and many of the staff, and contribute to the eclectic and sometimes chaotic style of practice which clearly informs and influences the built work.

Involvement in the arts and multiculturalism is complemented by Thomas and Peter Keller's research and activities for new housing types and forms, as well as their interest in participatory design processes. Ecology and green building

beiten zum Wohnungsbau und zu gemeinschaftlichen Entwurfsprozessen abgerundet. Ökologie und umweltbewusste Baumethoden, neue Finanzierungsmodelle im Wohnungsbau, Stadtplanung und die Schaffung von attraktivem Lebensraum sind Beispiele in einer Liste, die immer noch wächst.

Beeinflusst durch die breitgefächerten Interessen der Mitarbeiter, deckt die Art der Bauaufgaben das ganze Spektrum ab. Scheinbar widersprüchliche Projekte und Bauherren reichen von der konservativen Schweizerischen Nationalbank bis hin zu sozialen Experimenten im Wohnungsbau, umfassen Schulen, Kindergärten und Sendetürme, exklusive Reihenhaussiedlungen sowie Radiostudios.

Andere Berner Architekten haben äusserst durchdachte, bis ins letzte Detail geplante Wohnbauten geschaffen, schöne aber restriktive Welten, ohne Spielraum für individuellen Geschmack. Die Resultate der Bemühungen von arb in diesem Feld sind eine Mischung aus der eigenen umfassenden architektonischen Vision und den Wünschen der Bewohner. Die grossen Wohnkomplexe, die durch diesen humanen Ansatz entstanden sind, zeigen die klare Handschrift der Architekten, erlauben den Bewohnern aber die Entfaltung eines persönlichen Umfeldes in den privaten und halbprivaten Bereichen – jedoch nicht auf Kosten der öffentlichen Bereiche, diesen verdichteten städtischen Räumen, welche zur Bildung echter Gemeinschaft beitragen können.

Der Entwurf für die Erweiterung des Bun-

methods, inventive financial structures to provide housing, city planning, and the creation of livable communities round out a list of topics which is still growing. Influenced by the members' broad interests, the programmatic range of projects spans the spectrum of building tasks. Seemingly opposite projects and clients include the ultra-conservative National Bank of Switzerland and social experiments in housing developments: schools, kindergartens and broadcast towers, high-end townhouses and broadcast facilities.

Bernese architects have been designing housing down to the last detail, creating beautiful but highly restrictive environments, and leaving no room for individual tastes. arb's efforts in that field have resulted in a blend of the architect's overall vision, and the individual tenant's preferences. This humanistic approach has created large housing complexes which clearly show the unified handwriting of the designers but allow the inhabitants to create their own environment in the private and semi-private domains. This is never done at the expense of the public areas, which are dense urban spaces, contributing to the building of real communities.

Projects like the design for the expansion of the Swiss Parliament in Bern, with its dynamic and asymmetrical tower, are sharply different from the competing scheme. No stylistic concessions have been made to the classicist monumentality of the original building that was

deshauses in Bern, mit dem dynamischen und asymmetrischen Turm, unterscheidet sich deutlich vom anderen Vorschlag. Die klassizistische Monumentalität des Originalgebäudes wird nicht nachempfunden, wie im Entwurf von Mario Botta. Das Projekt ist wirklich modern, vermeidet die Falle der naheliegenden axialen Lösung und entwirft ein Bild der Schweiz das vorwärts- und nicht zurückgerichtet ist.

Durchdrungen von den Tugenden und der Seriosität der schweizerischen Architekturszene, besitzt arb doch den Witz und die Frechheit, die Regeln zu brechen. Die Weigerung, sich dem Dogma des Üblichen und Gewohnten zu unterwerfen, hat zu einer offenen Organisation geführt, die dort Möglichkeiten sieht, wo andere vor den Schwierigkeiten kapitulieren. Das zeigt sich in der Expansion in andere Gegenden der Welt und in neue Tätigkeitsgebiete. Durch die flexible Struktur scheint arb ausgezeichnet für eine neue Realität im Architekturbereich vorbereitet, die das traditionelle Verständnis ausdehnt und weder nationale noch kulturelle Grenzen kennt.

Tief verwurzelt in der Moderne, mit Vorgängern, die direkt von Le Corbusier zu Hans Brechbühler und zum Atelier 5 führen, hat arb trotzdem von den wertvolleren Lektionen der Postmoderne gelernt.

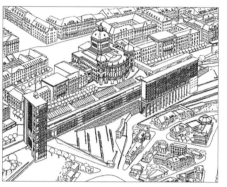

Bundeshaus

emulated in Mario Botta's schemes. The project is truly modern in spirit and avoids the pitfalls of a more obvious and boring axial solution, projecting an image for Switzerland that is looking to the future instead of the past.

Necessarily infused with the virtue of the gravely serious Swiss design business, arb nonetheless possesses the wit and audacity to break the rules and surprise with the unexpected. The refusal to adhere to the dogma of the prescribed party-line results in an organization that is truly open-ended and creates opportunities where the usual suspects would see problems and barriers.

This is made evident by the ongoing move into different regions of the world, and into developing aspects of the profession, which are still unexplored by most local firms. The flexible structure of the Arbeitsgruppe seems to position them perfectly for a new reality in the architectural design business, which includes a much broader understanding of the typical job description, and which knows no national or cultural borders.

Deeply rooted in Modernism, with ancestors that come straight from Le Corbusier to Hans Brechbühler and Atelier 5, arb has nonetheless absorbed some of the more valuable critical lessons of

Und zwar nicht in stilistischem Sinn, sondern in der Haltung und im praktischen Umgang. Mit einer erweiterten Vision der Aufgabe des Architekten, mit dem Einbezug des Multi-Kulturalismus und eines sozialen Bewusstseins und durch die erweiterte Definition des Funktionalismus hat arb sich vielleicht auf ein älteres Verständnis des modernen Architekten zurückbesonnen.

Basierend auf der Neugierde und dem Willen zu experimentieren und sich weiterzuentwickeln, ist diese Denkart sehr verschieden von der stilistischen Idee von «modern», die eine versteinerte und oberflächliche Tradition geworden ist. Der ganzheitliche Ansatz, welcher das Dogma überwindet, das jetzt sogar der modernen Tradition anhaftet, sollte die Arbeitsgruppe befähigen, sich auf eine noch schneller ändernde Welt vorzubereiten. Wir können darauf gespannt sein, wie sich das Werk von arb in bis jetzt noch unbekannte Gebiete vorwagen wird.

Ha Tinh, Vietnam

postmodern culture. Not in a stylistic sense, but with respect to attitude and approach to practice. By taking into account a broader vision of the architect's task, by including multiculturalism and a social conscience, and by expanding the definition of functionalism, perhaps arb has gone back to an earlier understanding of the modern architect.

Based on curiosity and a will to experiment and grow, this way of thinking is very different from the stylistic idea of modern, which has become a rigid and superficial tradition by itself. This inclusive approach, which bypasses the dogma now attached to even the modern tradition, should prepare the group for an ever faster changing world, and we can look forward to its oeuvre to expand into still uncharted territory.

EINE GUTE WOHNUNG

Lore Ditzen, Berlin

«Was hat man dem kleinen Mann

nicht alles versprochen: das Land Utopia,

den kommunistischen Zukunftsstaat,

das neue Jerusalem, selbst ferne Planeten.

Er aber wollte immer nur eins:

ein Haus mit Garten.»

Was der englische Romancier Gilbert K. Chesterton schon zu einer Zeit ironisierte, in der Ideologien noch Zukunft verhiessen, hat sich in unseren Tagen bewahrheitet: Immer mehr Menschen wollen – jedenfalls in unseren Breiten – zum gebauten Heim auch die frische Natur, sehr gern inmitten der Stadt. Das einschlägige Ideal hat der Satiriker Kurt Tucholsky im Berlin der zwanziger Jahre benannt: Man wünscht sich «vorn den Ku-Damm und hinten die Ostsee». Oder den Wald. Auf jeden Fall wollen wir tatsächlich beides – die reichhaltigen Angebote der Stadt und zugleich die Erholung davon. Und dazwischen den intimen Bereich des privaten Lebens: das Heim als Burg.

Alles zusammen ist mit dem Wort «Wohnen» gemeint, das heute vordergründig als Synonym für kreative Inneneinrichtung verstanden wird. Aber es erschöpft sich keineswegs in den Sitz- und Liegelandschaften, den rustikalen oder technischen Küchen und sonstigen «Wohnstilen» der Lifstyle-Magazine. Wohnen, Wohnung haben, meint nichts geringeres als auf dieser Erde zu Hause zu sein – im engeren wie im weiteren Sinn, der Ort und Landschaft, ferne Regionen und selbst den Himmel umfasst und alle Lebewesen beheimatet: «frösch wonen in lachen und weyern» heisst es nach Äsop im Mittelalter und: «in dieser Landschaft wohnen Elefanten, Rhinozerosse» lässt uns Brehms Tierleben wissen. Man kann schon seit dem 17. Jahrhundert «im wohnbar land Afrika», in einem durch Umbau «wohnbar gemachten Baurenhause», «auf dem Fluss» wohnen oder sich mit Lichtenberg vorstellen, dass wir «einige Meilen über die Erde wohnten», gar mit einem Herrn Reimarus die Ansicht teilen, dass «alle 6 Planeten wohnbare Erden» seien. Hier oder dort, in einem Gehäuse oder im

13

Kosmos oder «in Gott»: immer ist ein Geborgensein gemeint, in dem man gern auch «bleiben» möchte (eine weitere Bedeutung von «wohnen»). Wovon denn auch so schöne Wendungen zeugen, wie «in der Minne wohnen» und einander «beiwohnen».

Fürs Kosmische sind Architekten nicht zuständig, obwohl sie mit immer höheren Turmhäusern auch am Himmel zu kratzen versuchen. Aber alles, was sonst mit dem Wohnen gemeint ist, fällt in ihre Zuständigkeit; zumindest müssen sie die Bedingungen dafür schaffen, dass Menschen «friedlich bey und nebeneinander wonen» können, wie schon ein frommer Wunsch aus dem Jahr 1555 lautet. Sie haben es sich besonders in unserem Jahrhundert damit nicht leicht gemacht, seit die Lebensnot der kleinen Leute in ihr Blickfeld geriet, die mit vielköpfigen Familien in engen Stuben hausten und so etwas wie Ausstattung nicht kannten.

Wohnungsbau wurde zur grossen sozialen Aufgabe der Baukunst, die nun in Standards für Wohnungen der Vielen wetteiferte und damit zugleich – nach dem ersten Weltkrieg – hohe Ziele anstrebte. «Es liegt an uns, die Welt neu, menschlich zu gestalten», schrieb als einer der Wortführer der Kritiker Adolf Behne, und ein anderer Repräsentant des neuen Bauens, Hugo Häring, postulierte: «Wollen wir Forderungen stellen für die Gestaltfindung der Dinge, so müssen wir zunächst Forderungen stellen für die Gestaltfindung eines neuen Lebens, einer neuen Gesellschaft.» Man kann sie eigentlich alle zitieren, die Baumeister, die – immer unter der Maxime des ökonomisch vertretbaren, «kostensparenden» Bauens – neue Raumideen für die kleinste Einheit der Familie wie für die grosse Einheit einer Siedlung oder eines neuen Stadtquartiers entwarfen, Licht in die Stuben und Grün vor die Haustüren brachten.

Eine ganz neue Gesellschaft haben wir nicht bekommen, und auch der mächtige Impetus, mit dem sich ein ganzer Berufsstand politischen Zielen verschrieb, ist nicht mehr da; die grossen Siedlungen sind – noch immer als Orte des «Bleibens» bewährt – ins denkmalgepflegte Pensionsalter gekommen. Architektonische Leistungen machen in der öffentlichen Wertung heute als repräsentative Grossbauten im Verein mit Generalunternehmern Karriere und das Wohnen

14

ergiesst sich – oft genug – in geklonten Typenmodellen aus dem Häusle-Mu-
sterkatalog über die Landschaften. Stadt und Land werden austauschbar: Hoch-
häuser wandern ins Grüne aus, und parallel dazu griff die Erosion der Städte
als Wohnorte um sich. Vernachlässigte alte Häuser wurden durch gesichtslo-
se neue ersetzt, Büros und Kanzleien nahmen von Wohnungen Besitz: schlei-
chende Veränderungen, denen mit den klassischen Werkzeugen des Architekten – Entwerfen und Bauen – gar nicht beizukommen war. Und nicht zu reden
von den Verlusten, mit denen die Entwicklungen einhergingen: an ästhetischen
Qualitäten, an Vielfältigkeit und sinnlichen Reizen, auch an der Fülle alltäg-
lichen, normalen Lebens.

VIERMAL VERWANDTE PRÄGUNGEN: DIE ARCHITEKTUR-COMPAGNIE

Langer Anlauf an ein Ziel, das nicht nur als ein einzelner Punkt sichtbar wird,
sondern eher als Konglomerat. Wie kommt ein Architekt, der das Gewissen und
die Leitbilder der Moderne im Gepäck hat, mit den heutigen Gegebenheiten
zurecht? Antwort: er tut sich mit anderen zusammen. Hier zum Beispiel wurden es dann ihrer vier – und wenn man die Mitarbeiter aus der nächstjüngeren
Generation dazu nimmt, noch ein paar mehr. Viermal verwandte Prägungen und
professionelles Know-how plus unterschiedliche Erfahrungen, die als Mitgift
eingebracht wurden: so vervielfachen sich die Haltungen hinsichtlich baulicher
Qualität, räumlichen Dispositionen, gebotener Sparsamkeit und dessen, was
die Wohnsoziologen und Planer «Bedürfnisse» nennen, was aber, unter diversen Aspekten natürlich, insgesamt «Leben» heisst. Oder wir können, siehe
oben, auch «Wohnen» sagen.

Die Vier sind selber ungemein lebensfreundlich und dabei von ganz unterschiedlichem Temperament und Neigung, was sich auch in ihren Wohnungen
zeigt. Vielleicht erklärt sich daraus der gemeinsame räumliche Nenner ihrer
Arbeitsstätte. Die sieht aus wie ein Biberbau, mit einem Gefüge aus Gängen,
Räumen und Treppen in einem äusserlich ziemlich zernagten hölzernen Gehäuse von erkennbarer handwerklicher Qualität. Es ist ein von Arbeit bewohntes
Gebrauchsstück, hier und da umstandslos räumlich den Erfordernissen ange-

passt, in dem sich nirgends private Ansprüche wichtig machen, allenfalls Spurenelemente von individuellen Interessen. Und auf eine seltsame Weise bildet dieses simple alte Fuhrhaltereihaus etwas von dem ab, was diese Architekten in ihren Arbeiten anstreben: langfristige, vielfältige, veränderbare und gänzlich unprätentiöse Nutzbarkeit.

Viele Einzelerfahrungen versammeln sich in dieser Architektur-Compagnie arb: Einer, Kurt Aellen, steht für die besondere Faszination durch die Raumerkundungen der Moderne, wie sie – in humanitärer Gesinnung – die verehrten grossen Baumeister Le Corbusier und Mies van der Rohe auch im experimentellen Wohnungsbau (der Weissenhofsiedlung 1927 und Mies mit anderen in der «Wohnung für das Existenzminimum» 1931) erprobten. Dazu hat er die ingenieurmässige Baukunst aus der Zusammenarbeit mit dem Büro des grossen französischen Konstrukteurs Jean Prouvé in das Team eingebracht.

Mit ihm zusammen hat Thomas Keller sich auf mehrjährige Erforschung von «Wohnbedürfnissen» und die Fragen eingelassen, wie – bei begrenzten Mitteln – Architektur beschaffen sein soll, um dem Leben – und das heisst auch seinem benötigten Mobiliar und der mit den Lebensaltern und Familiengrössen wechselnden Nutzung – möglichst viel Spielraum zu schaffen. Ergebnis dieser Arbeit war das Wohnungs-Bewertungs-System (WBS), das als Richtschnur für Wohnungsbauförderung qualitative Massstäbe setzte. Wieder ein anderer, Peter Keller, hat sich besonders alter Häuser und ihrer «sanften» Erneuerung angenommen und die Frage der «Bedürfnisse» in den langwierigen, zermürbenden Prozessen der Mietermitsprache und mit den Mitteln der Profession beantwortet. Und Franz Biffiger – sozusagen das politische Gewissen seiner Zunft – hat sich jahrelang als Stadt- und Grossrat im Parlament und als Präsident der Kommission für Boden- und Mieterfragen der Schweizerischen Sozialdemokraten, um die Grundlagen dessen gekümmert, was Wohnen und Bleiben für das Lebensgefüge einer Kommune bedeutet: den Schutz innerstädtischer Häuser durch ein Abbruchgesetz, den Schutz ihrer Bewohner vor Vertreibung und Veränderung durch schieren Kommerz – und die Festlegung von Gebieten für bestimmte Nutzungen und gegen willkürlichen merkantilen Bodenverschleiss.

Auf eine seltsame Weise bildet dieses simple alte Fuhrhaltereihaus etwas von dem ab, was diese Architekten in ihren Arbeiten anstreben: langfristige, vielfältige, veränderbare und gänzlich unprätentiöse Nutzbarkeit.

16

Sie haben als Hochschullehrer oder in öffentlichen Gremien gewirkt. Sie haben Schulen und Kindergärten, Landwirtschaftsbetriebe und Verwaltungsbauten entworfen oder umgebaut, Nutzungs- und Gestaltungspläne konzipiert, an Entwicklungsprojekten in Ländern der dritten Welt gearbeitet. Und sie sind kontinuierlich mit dem Bauen von Wohnungen beschäftigt.

Zum Beispiel Siedlungen – die komplexeste Aufgabe. Dass die Ansprüche an die Wohnungen heute hoch sind, wissen wir aus der Wohnwert-Studie: man soll viel mit ihnen anfangen können. Man will nicht festgelegt sein bei der Einrichtung (was hohe Anforderungen an die Grundrisse stellt, vor allem auf beschränktem Raum) und schon gar nicht im Hinblick auf Anwachsen und Abnahme der Anzahl Familienmitglieder. Denn schliesslich heisst Wohnen auch dableiben wollen – vertraut sein mit der eigenen Umgebung, mit dem Ort, dem sozialen Geflecht.

EIN ORT, DER IMMER SCHON DA WAR: AUMATT

Die «Aumatt» (1973–1992) ist ein städtisches Dorf. Liegt in der Landschaft am Hang, zwischen Waldrand und Flusstal. Tut nicht – was bei Hangsiedlungen naheliegt und gern so gemacht wird – als wäre sie die Sonnenterrassenformation eines Sanatoriums. Sie hat nicht nur Aussen- sondern auch Innenbezüge: eine – autofreie – Hauptstrasse, Arkaden mit Bänken, überbaute Passagen, verschieden grosse Räume, Höfe und Plätze, Treppenwege und Pfade unter Terrassen und Hang-Gärtchen, eine «Arena» für Versammlungen und Aufführungen. Man kann sich in ihr bewegen wie in den Wallbereichen einer alten Stadt, in denen Gebautes und Natur sich verschränken. Die Häuser haben Zugang vom «städtischen» Strassengefüge und Ausgänge durch Terrassentreppen und Gärtchen. Sie sind von heute. Hier waltet formal keine Sentimentalität, die sich in dekorativen Zugeständnissen äussert, sondern «zeitlose» Modernität. Ihre spezielle Qualität liegt im Variantenreichtum des Umgangs mit dem Raum, drinnen und draussen.

Raum misst sich nicht nur in Quadratmetern; er wird auch durch Licht gewonnen, das hereingeholt wird auf vielfältige Weise: über Terrassen, Loggien, Glas-

dächer. Loggien sind manchmal ganz klein, treten in spitzen Winkeln aus der Hauswand vor, fangen das Licht von zwei Seiten ein und erlauben ebenso Ausblick in die Umgebung. Man kann da sitzen, ruhen und schauen, wie Goethe im – hölzernen – Geräms seiner Kindheit.

Raum wird gewonnen auch durch die Art der Einbauten: Treppen sind innen und aussen leicht, aus Gitterstahl, der – durchsichtig – den Raum nicht verstellt; Handläufe aus Stahlrohr liegen gut in der Hand. Balkonbrüstungen aus Lochstahl, der Fäden von Helligkeit in die Räume spinnt. «Raumdisposition» ist einer der wichtigsten «Wohnwerte», die die Forschungsarbeit von arb ergab; sie ist, zusammen mit «Licht», eine der Maximen der Architekten geblieben. Immer spielt dabei der ökonomische Aspekt eine Rolle, denn das Wohnen soll zwar gut, darf aber nicht teuer sein.

Sparsamkeit bestimmt die überlegte Auswahl von Materialien und die langfristige Tauglichkeit der Wohnungen: sie ist, im wörtlichen Sinne, der Boden der Bauten von arb.

Sparsamkeit bestimmt die überlegte Auswahl von Materialien und die langfristige Tauglichkeit der Wohnungen: sie ist, im wörtlichen Sinne, der Boden der Bauten von arb. Eine eigens für die Aumatt gegründete Genossenschaft erlaubte günstigen Bodenerwerb, dessen finanzielle Vorteile dem gesamten Projekt zugute kamen. Genossenschaften machen keine Bodenspekulationsgewinne. Auch «Merzenacker», ein weiteres Siedlungsprojekt, hat dank der von der arb gegründeten genossenschaftlichen Bauherrschaft seinen Baugrund günstig erwerben und so die Baukosten senken können.

Genossenschaft heisst auch «Bindung»: Beteiligung an der Planung, Anspruch auf Berücksichtigung individueller Wünsche, Absprachen für das soziale Miteinander. Die Siedlung wuchs wie ein Dorf: nicht auf einmal aus der Retorte, sondern in aufeinanderfolgenden «Hofgemeinschaften», die für ihre Umgebung gemeinschaftlich Verantwortung tragen und durchaus auch Konflikte auszuhalten haben, wie sie sich aus den kontrastierenden Ansprüchen von Öffentlichkeit und Privatheit ergeben. Gemeinschaftseinrichtungen sorgen für Kontakte und geteilte Aufgaben: Mehrzweck- und Jugendräume, Spielplätze, Fahrradwerkstatt, Boule-Bahn und Spielhalle am grossen Platz, auf dem auch Feste stattfinden, Wasserplanschbecken und stille Teichgewässer in einem «versunkenen Garten». Die Architekten haben auch mit den Ohren gebaut: Gummibe-

lag dämpft den Lärm auf Spielfeldern, Holzverkleidung den unter Strassen-
passagen. Oben am Waldrand bilden Gemüsebeete und Sträucher verschiedener Eigentümer einen gemeinschaftlichen Nutzgarten. Was in der Siedlung an
Grünem wächst, ist – landschaftsgärtnerisch eingebrachte – Wildnatur: ein weiterer Beitrag zur Integration des Ortes in seine Umgebung. Hier wurde nur angelegt, was die Region an Pflanzenwuchs selber gedeihen lässt. Walnuss- und
Vogelbeerbaum, Wildkirsche und Weide wachsen zwischen den Häusern. Aber
für den Feigenbaum auf einem sonnigen Aussenraumfleck in einer Mauernische
ist, wie hie und da in den Individualbereichen für andere Pflanzen, auch noch
Platz. Mit ihren Wildgärten, Bäumen und begrünten Dächern zieht sich die Aumatt unauffällig in die Umgebung zurück. Sie wirkt wie ein Ort, der immer schon
da war – und das ist das, was ihren Architekten am besten gefällt.

GRÖSSTE FREIHEIT IN DER BENÜTZUNGSART: MERZENACKER

Man kann das sogar auch vom «Merzenacker» (1974–1987) sagen – einer ganz
anderen Anlage im Vorfeld der Stadt und sozusagen auf der grünen Wiese. Von
weitem ist sie ein blosser Fleck in der Landschaft, kaum wahrnehmbar in der
entfernteren Nachbarschaft etlicher hochgestellter Wohnkisten am Fuss eines
Hügels. Im Näherkommen denkt man an Treibhäuser: graues Stahlblech und
viel Glas, das hält die Landschaft vor dem fernen Horizont der Alpenkulisse gut
aus. Es ist ein bescheidenes Konzentrat von Räumen, die sich nicht wichtig machen. Erst ganz aus der Nähe und dann vor allem drinnen offenbart sich die
räumliche Opulenz, die sich teilweise unterm grauen Blechmantel versteckt
und allenfalls mit reichlichen Glasfensterkörpern auf ihr interessantes Innen-
leben verweist.

«Drinnen» ist die Siedlung grösser, als man von weitem ahnt – mit einer breit-
räumigen Strasse, an der auch Ateliers und der Kindergarten liegen, und mit
grösseren Vorgartenräumen, deren Abgrenzungsgestänge mit der Zeit unter
grünem Gerank verschwinden sollen. Den «kostengünstigen spartanischen
Umgang mit der Baustruktur», wie ein arb-Architekt sagt, sieht man der Vielfalt von räumlichen Elementen nicht an. Es gibt Grundriss- und Haustypen unter-

*Im Näher-
kommen denkt
man an Treib-
häuser: graues
Stahlblech und
viel Glas, das
hält die Land-
schaft vor dem
fernen Horizont
der Alpen-
kulisse gut
aus. Es ist ein
bescheidenes
Konzentrat von
Räumen, die
sich nicht wich-
tig machen.*

19

schiedlicher Grössenordnung mit unterschiedlichen Standards – auch sehr einfachen – und dann die immens grosszügigen zweigeschossigen Häuser, die nebeneinander an einem glasüberdachten Gang liegen und von oben bis unten einen einzigen Raum zu bilden scheinen. Hier konnte sich für die individuellen Bauherren der Genossenschaft der Architektentraum verwirklichen: ein variables System zu errichten, das Jedem räumliche Anordnungen nach eigenem Gusto erlaubt.

Keine Wohnung ist wie die andere – und auch spätere Umbaumöglichkeiten werden rege genutzt. Man spürt die Präsenz der grossen Vorbilder dieser Architekten, z.B. Mies van der Rohes. Dieser liesse sich hier wörtlich zitieren: «Wirtschaftliche Gründe fordern Rationalisierung und Typisierung. Auf der anderen Seite fordert die immer steigende Differenzierung unserer Wohnbedürfnisse grösste Freiheit in der Benützungsart. Es wird in Zukunft notwendig sein, beiden Tendenzen gerecht zu werden. Der Skelettbau ist hierzu das geeignetste Konstruktionssystem. Er ermöglicht eine rationelle Herstellung und lässt der inneren Raumaufteilung jede Freiheit. Beschränkt man sich darauf, lediglich Küche und Bad ihrer Installationen wegen als konstante Räume auszubilden und entschliesst man sich dann noch, die übrige Wohnfläche mit verstellbaren Wänden aufzuteilen, so glaube ich, dass mit diesen Mitteln jedem berechtigten Wohnanspruch genügt werden kann.»

Auch für das Nebeneinander bescheidener und grosszügiger Wohnungen an einem Ort hätte Mies die passende Antwort parat – wie er sie anlässlich seiner beiden Entwürfe zur Ausstellung der «Wohnung für das Existenzminimum» 1931 in Berlin Kritikern entgegenhielt. «Das Problem der neuen Wohnung ist ein geistiges Problem und der Kampf um die neue Wohnung der Kampf um neue Lebensformen.»

Keine Wohnung wie die andere, mehr oder weniger «durchsichtig» alle. Das setzt natürlich Übereinkünfte der Familienmitglieder, bestimmte Verhaltensweisen voraus. Die Küche als Anordnung halbhoher Tresen zum Beispiel, mit gleichzeitigen Blickkontakten in Ober- und Untergeschoss und auf die Treppe. Die Treppe aus Gitterstahl, durchsichtig wie die drahtseilbespannten Brü-

20

stungen. Nicht jedermanns Sache dürfte es sein, allenthalben weissen Flie-
senboden zu haben – aber hier gibt es eben keinerlei Jedermann. Jede Wohnung ist überraschend anders in ihrer Grosszügigkeit – und das Tageslicht, das
hier erst recht eine raumgreifende Rolle spielt, darf einmal sogar die Glaska-
chelwände eines Badezimmers durchdringen, das die Bewohner frei in den
Raum stellten.

Die Materialien sind bei den Häusern von arb fast überall dieselben: einfach
und sorgfältig verarbeitet – und man trifft sie nicht nur in diesen Gebäuden an,
die ihre Opulenz im Understatement verbergen, sondern zum Beispiel auch bei
einem sehr geliebten Projekt, das dem Engagement der Moderne im «Bauen
für das Existenzminimum» vergleichbar ist. Heute hat sich dieses Engagement
vor allem in der Erfüllung von Wohnbedürfnissen innerhalb unzulänglicher Altbauten zu bewähren.

HÄUSER WIEDER LEBENSTÜCHTIG MACHEN: OBERES MURIFELD

Auch die Erneuerungsaufgabe im «Oberen Murifeld» (1995–1997) gilt Genos-
senschaftsbauten. Was in den zwanziger Jahren sozialer Fortschritt war, ist heute, angesichts fortentwickelter Standards, unzulänglich geworden und über-
dies durch Vernachlässigung seitens der Eigentümer – in diesem Fall die Stadt
– zusätzlich heruntergekommen. Die 200 Wohnungen in den Miethäusern der
immer noch schönen Gesamtanlage hatten weder Bäder noch Zentralheizung
und keine Balkone. arb und einem anderen Architekten-Team fiel die Aufgabe
zu, in einem Pilotprojekt die Häuser wieder lebenstüchtig zu machen – und
zwar in Abstimmung mit den Mietern und deren divergierenden Wünschen, der
ökonomischen Vertretbarkeit und den architektonischen Möglichkeiten.
Wer die Kämpfe und Auseinandersetzungen um menschenwürdiges Wohnen
im Altbau aus den siebziger und achtziger Jahren noch in Erinnerung hat, der
weiss auch, was Architekten auf sich nehmen, die sich für diese Aufgabe en-
gagieren. Man weiss aber auch, dass ihre Lösung sich nicht auf die Wohnzu-
friedenheit der Mieter beschränkt (die neuen Bäder und Balkone – oder das
Schwimmbad im Haus und den Garten im Hof), sondern dass damit auch ein

Beitrag zur Erhaltung der Stadt geleistet wird. Häuser und Menschen sind Zeugen und Teilhaber ihrer Geschichtlichkeit und ihres Charakters, Bestandteile ihrer urbanen Vielfalt und damit ihrer Lebendigkeit und Attraktivität. Nur in der Erhaltung – und durch die Gestaltung – dieser Zusammenhänge kann auch die Stadt «eine gute Wohnung» sein, für alles, was sich kontrastierend in ihr an Lebensansprüchen und -zwecken regt.

Die Arbeitsbegriffe dafür heissen «Stadterneuerung» – «sanft» oder «behutsam»; die Wahrung dieser Zusammenhänge steht für das, was die Architekten von arb mit «Ökologie» meinen. Die Grundlagen für diese Arbeit mussten politisch geschaffen werden – wie zum Beispiel mit der oben genannten Gesetzgebung, die Franz Biffiger durchsetzen half.

Die Reitschule ist geradezu ein Modellbeispiel für den Verfall, die Neubewertung und Umnutzung historischer Bauten. Diese Aufgabe reicht weit hinaus über den bis dahin geltenden Denkmalschutzbegriff, der nur Einzelgebäude mit anerkannter historischer Bausubstanz betraf.

RAUM FÜR ENTWICKLUNGEN FREIHALTEN: BERNER REITSCHULE

Dass die arb sich mit ihrer sozialen und kommunikativen Orientierung als unabdingbarem Qualitätsbestandteil ihres professionellen Selbstverständnisses auf die langwierige Erhaltungs- und Erneuerungsproblematik der alten Berner Reitschule (seit 1982) einliess, nimmt also nicht Wunder.

Die Reitschule ist geradezu ein Modellbeispiel für den Verfall, die Neubewertung und Umnutzung historischer Bauten, wie sie sich seit den siebziger Jahren überall in Europa als herausfordernde Aufgabe präsentierten. Diese Aufgabe reicht weit hinaus über den bis dahin (d.h. etwa bis zum Europäischen Denkmalschutzjahr 1975) geltenden Denkmalschutzbegriff, der nur Einzelgebäude mit anerkannter historischer Bausubstanz betraf. Ins Blickfeld rückten Ensemble und Quartier, räumliche und soziale Zusammenhänge; der qualitative und ästhetische Wert alter Baustrukturen wie ökonomische und soziale Aspekte ihrer Erhaltung. Für neue Nutzungen aufgegebener Bauten hatten einfallsreiche Gruppen junger Leute vielgestalten Bedarf: Musikmachen, Theaterspielen, Tanzen, Sich-Treffen, Organisieren und Ausleben von Selbsthilfe- und Polit-Aktivitäten und viel Anderes mehr: Das Buch über den Zusammenhang zwischen Umnutzung verlassener Gebäude und selbstbestimmt sich entfaltender neuer Kreativität wäre noch zu schreiben: leere Fabriken, alte Müh-

22

len, nutzlose Bauernhöfe, verrottende Bergwerksanlagen; für Bern liegt es, herausgegeben von den Betreibern der Reitschule, bereits vor.

In Bern wurde die Reitschule zum Magneten solcher Bewegungen. Wie überall auch, waren ihre Anlagen – Reithalle, Remisen, Wohngebäude – erst einmal vom kommunalen Eigentümer dem Verfall preisgegeben, bis Akteure von ihr Besitz ergriffen, und – zunächst illegal, dann geduldet – aus eigenen Kräften notdürftig Instandhaltung betrieben. Die Stadt als Eigentümerin liess anfallsweise flicken – aber das Gutachten, das die arb in ihrem Auftrag vorlegte, wies Dächer, Türen und Fenster, Toiletten, Heizungen und Abwasserleitungen als beschädigt oder unzulänglich aus. Erst 5 Jahre später gab es, für Teilnutzungen durch die Stadt (AJZ), erste provisorische Instandsetzungen, dann (1997) ein neues Erneuerungs- und Nutzungskonzept, das den inzwischen dort angesiedelten lebendigen Aktivitäten Rechnung trug. In Ställen, Remisen und Wohngebäuden gibt es ein Restaurant, Veranstaltungsräume, Druckerei und Fotolabor, Kino und Werkstätten, Frauenraum und Wohngemeinschaft; die grosse Halle steht als Veranstaltungs- und Arbeitsort auch anderen Unternehmungen offen.

Die Arbeit der arb ist darauf gerichtet, diesen Betrieb zu erhalten und zu sichern. Für die Sanierungsaufgabe bedeutet das: «behutsame Erneuerung» – so wenig Eingriffe wie möglich, diese aber nachhaltig und dauerhaft. Nutzungsneutrale Räume schaffen, die zukünftige Entwicklungen nicht determinieren. Prozesshaft – d.h. stufenweise – vorgehen und die einzelnen Schritte abstimmen.

Vorbild für diese Art der schrittweisen, gemeinsam verantworteten Erneuerung, die Raum für Entwicklungen freihält, ist die «Bauhütte». Allgemeines Nutzungsziel ist eine «gedeckte Allmend», die neben den ständigen Einrichtungen offen für möglichst breite Kreise ist – vor allem die Reithalle selbst. In diesem Projekt ist arb seit 16 Jahren engagiert. Seine Durchführung steht erst am Anfang. Die erste Sanierungsetappe, die 1999 mit der Dachrenovation beginnt, wird auf 3 bis 4 Jahre berechnet.

Einen ganz anderen Aspekt der Stadterneuerung repräsentiert die Aufgabe, die sich mit dem Um- und Anbau der Fernmeldedirektion (1980–1992), aus den fünfziger Jahren, inmitten der Stadt ergab. Altbau und Neubauten waren zu verbinden, mit Verwaltungserweiterung und Wohnhäusern ein Block, der als Strassendreieck auf das Kräftefeld der Umgebung Rücksicht zu nehmen hat. Das besteht aus Bauten von sehr unterschiedlichem Alter und Proportionen – von 100jährigen Giebelhäusern bis zu den ausgedehnten Horizontalstaffelungen gegenwärtigen Bauens. Die Architektur von arb antwortet darauf mit raffinierter Unauffälligkeit: additiven Fensterschlitzen, die die Fenstermasse des Altbaus spannungsvoll ergänzen und Vertikalbetonungen und Proportionen aus der Umgebung aufnehmen – mit der schwungvollen Verbindung von Alt- und Neubau. Oder hier nun auch mit der diskreten, horizontal und vertikal geometrisch gegliederten Farbigkeit der Fassadengestaltung, in der sich die Farben des Quartiers andeutend wiederfinden: ein rosafarbenes Grau, ein sandiges Weiss, eine Ahnung von Grün – hier aber nicht in totem Putz, sondern in der Lebendigkeit natürlichen Kalksteins.

Das repräsentative Objekt hat Geld – und es hat viel Zeit gekostet, als die Baugenehmigung sich um zwei Jahre verzögerte. Hier nun konnte sich einmal, erzwungenermassen aber mit ungehemmtem Vergnügen, die ästhetische Lust eines Architekten ausleben, als der zuständige arb-Architekt Kurt Aellen sich auf die langwierige Steinsuche machte. Mitgebracht hat er für Fensterfassungen, Platten und Vertikalstreifen nicht nur die farblich stimmigen Kalksteine französischer Provinzen, sondern auch deren beste Weinsorten, die er genüsslich mit Namen nennt. Oder vielleicht war es auch umgekehrt: dass ihm der Wein den Weg zu den Steinen wies. Jedenfalls steht auch der Lavasockel aus dem italienischen Orvieto mit dem dortigen Gewächs in urschöpferischem Zusammenhang. So ist das feine Zeugnis einer repräsentativen städtischen Erneuerung entstanden, mit den Finessen seines wertvollen Understatements so unauffällig selbstverständlich, dass es wie ein längst integrierter Bestandteil der Stadt wirkt. Auf die Finessen der Details in Fensterprofilierungen, Rah-

menverstärkungen und -verschlankungen macht Kurt Aellen immer wieder nachdrücklich aufmerksam; es sind Spezialitäten des arb-Mitarbeiters Laurent Cantalou – «unseres architektonischen Gewissens».

Anderes spricht, unaufdringlich, beim Durchgang durch die Gebäude für sich: wie im Treppenhaus Alt- und Neubau zusammengeführt werden, wie Fensterdurchbrüche im Altbau mit neuen Fenstern im Neubau korrespondieren, wie Oberlichtfenster in Korridoren die Räume erweitern, Halbsäulen die Länge der Korridore gliedern und optisch verkürzen helfen. Wie eine Milchglasscheibe am Ende eines Korridors den Dachgarten des niedrigeren alten Hauses gegenüber mit der Intimität des Sonnenstuhls, der Trockenwäsche, der Katze, vor Einsicht schützt. Umsicht vom Feinsten; sie reicht bis in die Blumenkästen aus dem gängigen Lochgitterstahl im leichten Gestänge und eingezogenen Rankdrähten, die in der Hauscafeteria den Buffetgang von den Restauranttischen trennen. «Mit Blumenkästen», zitiert Aellen trübe Erfahrungen von Kollegen, «wird meistens nachträglich räumlich viel ruiniert». Hier sind sie Teil der Architektur.

Wo wohnen wir? Auch in den Arbeitsstätten, den öffentlichen Einrichtungen unserer Orte. In den Strassen der Stadt, im Anblick der Häuser, die unsere Blicke halten oder ermüden lassen. Im Reichtum ihrer Vielfalt, der uns Spielraum für Leben gewährt. Unser Anspruch auf eine «gute Wohnung» endet nicht an der Haus- oder Gartentür.

A GOOD PLACE FOR LIVING

Lore Ditzen, Berlin

"What hasn't been promised to the small man?

The land of Utopia, the communist future state,

the New Jerusalem, even the distant planets.

But he always wanted just one thing:

A house with a garden."

What the English novelist Gilbert K. Chesterton ironically wrote about during a time when ideologies were still promising a bright future for all has become true in our time: an increasing number of people—at least in our region—want fresh nature with their home, and in many cases in the center of the city. The satirist Kurt Tucholsky described the relevant ideal in the Berlin of the twenties: what was wished for was "Kurfürstendamm out front and the Baltic Sea in the back." Or the forest. At any rate, we do want both—the comprehensive offerings of the city and, at the same time, a respite from it. And in between, the intimate realm of private life: the home as castle.

The term "living," which today is superficially understood as a synonym for creative interior design, refers to all of the above. But it's not at all limited to chair and sofa landscapes, rustic or technical kitchens, or any of the other "interior design styles" of the lifestyle magazines. Living, having a home, means nothing less than having a home on this earth—in the narrower and broader sense, comprising location and landscape, distant regions, and even the sky, housing all living beings. "Frogs live in puddles and ponds" is what Aesop said in the Middle Ages, and what we learn from Brehm's Tierleben is that "in this landscape live elephants and rhinoceroses." Since the seventeenth century we've been able to live "in the habitable land of Africa," in a "farmhouse made habitable" by conversion, "on the river." Or we can imagine, from Lichtenberg, to "live a couple of miles above the earth," or we can share the opinion with Mr. Reimarus that "all 6 planets are inhabitable." Here and there, in a housing structure of one form or another or in the cosmos or "in God," what is al-

ways meant is a feeling of security in which one wants to "stay" (another meaning of "living").

Architects are not in charge of the cosmos, although they try to scratch the sky with ever-taller skyscrapers. But everything else that is meant by "living" is their responsibility; at least, they have to create the conditions for people to "live peacefully together and next to each other," as a wishful thought from 1555 goes. Especially in our century, they haven't made it easy for themselves, ever since the misery of the "ordinary people," who lived with large families in cramped rooms and knew nothing about interior design, entered their field of vision.

Housing became the big social task for architects, who now competed for the development of housing standards for the masses and, simultaneously, after World War I, set for themselves ever-higher goals. "It is up to us to redesign the world in a new and humane way," wrote the critic Adolf Behne as one of the premier spokesmen. And another representative of the new architecture, Hugo Häring, postulated: "If we want to set standards for the design of things, we first have to set standards for the design of a new life, a new society." Really, all of the architects who—always under the maxim of the economically justifiable, "cost-saving" building—designed new spatial ideas for both the smallest family unit and for the large unit of a development or a new urban quarter, who brought light into the rooms and green outside the front doors, could be quoted.

We didn't get a totally new society, and the mighty impetus that inspired an entire profession to devote itself to idealistic political goals is no longer there; the large developments—still accepted as places for "staying"—have entered their historically preserved retirement age. In today's evaluation, architectural achievements make a career for themselves as representative large-scale buildings in collaboration with general contractors, and "living" pours often enough into the landscapes in cloned archetypes from the catalog. City and country become interchangeable, high-rise buildings move into the country and, simultaneously, the erosion of the cities as places to live spreads out from

the core. Old, neglected houses were replaced by faceless new ones, offices took possession of apartments: creeping changes that couldn't be gotten at with the classical tools of the architect—designing and building. Not to mention the losses accompanying the developments: in aesthetic qualities, in variety and sensual stimuli, also in the wealth of the everyday normal life.

Four Related Characters: The Architektur Compagnie

A long arduous path to a goal that becomes visible, not as an individual point but rather as a conglomerate. How does an architect who is carrying with himself the conscience and archetypes of Modernism cope with today's conditions? Answer: he gets together with others. In this case, there were four, and if we add the employees from the following generation, there are a few more. Four related characters and professional know-how plus different experiences that were entered as dowries: this is how the attitudes toward architectural quality multiply—toward spatial dispositions, appropriate austerity and toward what the sociologists and planners call "needs," which, under many different aspects, of course, means "life." Or we can also say, as above, "living."

In a strange way this simple old coach house displays something of what these architects try to achieve with their work: longterm, variable, manifold and completely unpretentious usability.

The four themselves have an incredible zest for life and they are of very different temperament and inclination, as can be seen in their apartments. Perhaps this explains the common spatial denominator of their workplace. It looks like a beaver hut, with an arrangement of hallways, spaces and stairs in a wooden structure that looks pretty well chewed up but displays a high level of craftsmanship. It is an object of use inhabited by work and workers, here and there simply adjusted to the requirements. Personal standards are not important in it, and only traces of individual interests are discernable. And in a strange way this simple old coach house displays something of what these architects try to achieve with their work: long-term, variable, manifold and completely unpretentious usability.

The experiences of four individuals are gathered in this Architektur Compagnie arb: one of them, Kurt Aellen, represents the special fascination for the spatial explorations of Modernism that were explored—with a humanitarian con-

viction—by two greatly admired architects Le Corbusier and Mies van der Rohe, also in experimental housing (Le Corbusier in the Weissenhof development
1927, and Mies van der Rohe, with others, in the "apartment for the subsistence level" 1931). For this, Aellen contributed the engineered architecture from
his collaboration with the office of the great French constructor, Jean Prouvé,
to the team.

Together with Aellen, Thomas Keller explored the "housing needs" for several years and the questions about how—given limited financial means—architecture should be designed to provide life. And this also refers to the furniture
required and a utilization that changes with age and family size—with as much
elbowroom as possible. The result of these efforts was a housing value study
that set qualitative standards as a guideline for state-sponsored housing. Yet
another, Peter Keller, devoted himself especially to old houses and their "soft"
renewal, and answered the question of "need" in the protracted, grueling law-
suits of tenants' rights using the means of the profession. And Franz Biffiger,
as a city and cantonal councilor in the Parliament and as a President for the
Commission for Ground and Tenants' Questions with the Swiss Social Demo-
crats—the political conscience of his guild, as it were—has for years cared for
the foundation of what living and staying means for the life structure in a community—the protection of inner-city houses through a demolition law, the protection of their inhabitants from eviction and from changes due to mere com-
mercialism, and the standardization of areas for certain uses and against the
arbitrary, mercantile wear and tear of the land.

They were all active as college teachers or as members in public bodies of ex-
perts. They designed or converted schools and kindergartens, agricultural businesses and administrative buildings, they conceived utilization and design
plans and worked on development projects in third world countries. And they
continuously deal with building apartments.

For example, housing developments – the most complex task. We know from
the housing value study that the standards for apartments are high today: they
should also be flexible. People don't want to be fixed with respect to furnish-

ing (which places high demands on the ground plans, and especially on limited availability of space), and certainly not with respect to the growth and decrease of the number of family members. After all, living also means wanting to stay—being familiar with one's own environment, with the location and with the social network.

A Place That Has Always Been There: Aumatt

The Aumatt (1973–1992) is an urban village. It's situated on a slope in the landscape, between the edge of the forest and the river valley. It doesn't pretend – the obvious and frequently practiced thing – as though it were the sun terrace of a sanatorium. It not only has relationships with the outside but also the inside: a car-free main road, arcades with benches, covered passageways, various large rooms, yards and squares, staircases and paths beneath terraces and the small hill gardens, an "arena" for meetings and events. One can move through it like through the bulwark areas of an old city, where architecture and nature interlock. The houses are accessible from the "urban" street network and can be exited via terrace stairs and small gardens. They are contemporary. Here, sentimentality is not expressed in decorative compromises but in "timeless" modernity. Their special quality is the wealth of variation in how space is dealt with, both inside and out.

Space isn't just measured in square meters; it is also created by light that is brought inside in different ways: via terraces, loggias, glass roofs. Loggias are, at times, very small; they emerge in acute angles from the house wall, catch the light from two sides and also allow for a view into the surrounding environment. You can sit there, rest and watch, just like Goethe in the—wooden— Geräms of his childhood.

Space is also gained through the type of installation: stairways are light both inside and out, made of metal gridwork that can be looked through and doesn't obstruct the space; tubular steel handrails feel comfortable in the hand. Balustrades made of perforated sheet metal that allows streams of light into the rooms. "Spatial disposition" is one of the most important "housing val-

ues" resulting from the research done by arb; together with "light," it is still one of the architects' axioms. Economics always plays a role because living should be good but not expensive.

Economics determine the careful selection of materials and long-term suitability of the apartments: it is, literally, the basis for arb's buildings. A cooperative founded especially for Aumatt allowed for the low-priced purchase of the land; the financial advantages benefited the entire project. Cooperatives don't make any profit on land speculation. "Merzenacker," another development project, was also able to purchase its land at a favorable price, thus lowering the building cost, thanks to the cooperative client founded by arb.

Cooperative also means "commitment": participation in the planning, the right to the consideration of individual wishes, arrangements for social cohabitation. The development grew like a village: not in one try from the test tube but in subsequent "farm communities" having a common responsibility for their environment and, quite possibly, also having to withstand conflicts that result from the contrasting standards of public and private life. Community institutions provide contacts and shared responsibilities: multipurpose- and youth-rooms, playgrounds, bicycle workshop, Boule courts and a game hall at the large square where festivities are held, rowing ponds and "silent" ponds in a "sunk garden." The architects also used their ears for the design: rubber coating cushions the noise on the playgrounds, wooden cladding muffles the noise below street passages. Above, at the edge of the forest, vegetable gardens and shrubs from different owners form a common garden. And the plants growing in the development are a bits of "wild" nature that were added through landscaping—another contribution to the integration of the site into its environment. Only plants that are indigenous to the region were planted here. Walnut, rowan, wild cherry and willow grow between the houses. But there is also space for the occasional fig tree in a sunny spot in a wall niche and, here and there, for other plants in individual areas. With its wild gardens, trees and planted roofs, Aumatt discretely submerges into the environment. It looks like a place that has always been there—and this is what the architects like best about it.

Economics determine the careful selection of materials and long-term suitability of the apartments: it is, literally, the basis for arb's buildings.

32

Largest Freedom of Use: Merzenacker

This can even be said of "Merzenacker" (1974–1987), a completely different complex outside of the city and, so to speak, in the green meadow. From a distance, it is a mere speck in the landscape, hardly noticeable in the more distant neighborhood of several tall housing blocks at the foot of a hill. As one approaches, an image of greenhouses arises: gray sheet metal and lots of glass, the landscape in front of the Alps on the distant horizon can stand up to it very well. It is a modest concentration of spaces that do not place themselves in the spotlight. Only from close-up and, above all, from inside the spatial opulence, which sometimes hides beneath a coat of gray sheet metal and may point to its interesting inner life only through abundant glass window volumes, does it reveal itself.

As one approaches, an image of greenhouses arises: gray sheet metal and lots of glass, the landscape in front of the Alps on the distant horizon can stand up to it very well.

"Inside," the development is larger than one would suspect from a distance—with a wide street seamed by studios and the kindergarten, and with larger front yards whose enclosing rod fences (now still irritatingly naked) are destined to disappear beneath green climbing plants. The "economical, Spartan handling of the building structure," as one of the arb architects says, can't be detected in the variety of spatial elements. There are ground plans and house types of different sizes with different standards—including very simple ones—and then the immensely generous two-story houses that are situated next to each other along a glass-covered walkway and seem to form a single space from top to bottom. Here, the architect's dream could be realized for the individual clients of the cooperative: erecting a flexible system that provides each individual with the spatial opportunity for arrangements according to his own taste.

No two apartments are alike, and the possibility for a later conversion is actively used. The presence of one of the great examples for these architects, Mies van der Rohe, can be felt here. He could be quoted literally: "Economic reasons require rationalization and typification. On the other end of the spectrum, the continuously increasing differentiation of our housing needs requires more freedom for its use. In the future, it will be necessary to do justice to both

33

tendencies. The skeleton building is the most appropriate construction system to do so. It allows for a rational production and leaves every freedom to the interior spatial arrangement. If we restrict ourselves to design only the kitchen and bathroom as constant spaces, due to the necessary plumbing installations, and if we then decide to divide the remaining floor space with adjustable walls, then I believe that every just housing standard can be met with these means." Mies van der Rohe also had the proper answer for the juxtaposition of modest and generous apartments in a single location—as he countered critics at the occasion of his two designs for the exhibition of the "apartment for the subsistence level" in Berlin in 1931. "The problem of the new apartment is a spiritual problem, and the fight for the new apartment is the fight for new forms of living."

No two apartments alike, all of them more or less "transparent." Of course, this presumes agreements between the family members and certain behaviors. The kitchen as an arrangement of half-height counters, for example, and visual contact with the upper and lower floor and the stairs. The metal grid staircase, transparent like the balustrades of tensioned cable. It may not be everybody's thing to have white tiles on the floor—but here, there is no anybody. Each apartment is surprisingly different in its generosity—and the daylight that plays a special spatial role here may even shine through the glass block walls of a bathroom that the inhabitants placed freely into the space.

The materials used in arb's houses are almost the same everywhere: simple and carefully processed—and we don't just find them in these buildings that hide their opulence in understatement but, for example, also in a very well-liked project that can be compared with Modernism's commitment to the "building for the subsistence level." Today, this commitment has to prove itself mainly in fulfilling the housing needs within insufficient old buildings.

REDESIGNING HOUSES TO COPE WITH LIFE: OBERES MURIFELD

The renewal task in "Oberes Murifeld" (1995–1997) is also dedicated to cooperative buildings. What was social progress during the twenties has today be-

come insufficient given the continuously evolving standards and has additionally gone to seed due to neglect by the owners – in this case, the town. The 200 apartments in the rental buildings of the complex, which still looks beautiful, had neither bathrooms nor central heat, nor balconies. arb and an other team of architects were given the task, within the framework of a pilot project, to make the houses suitable for living—in accordance with the tenants' wishes, the economic feasibility and the architectural possibilities.

Those who remember the battles and debates from the seventies and eighties about living in old buildings in a way fit for human beings know the weight architects who commit themselves to this task take upon their shoulders. But we also know that their solution isn't limited to satisfying the tenants (they wish for and get, for example, bathrooms and balconies – or the swimming pool in the house and the garden in the yard), but that they also make a contribution towards the preservation of the town. Houses and people are witnesses and participants to a towns history and character, elements of its urban variety and thus its liveliness and appeal. Only through the preservation—and design—of these contexts can the city be "a good place to live" for everything that moves in it in terms of living standard and purpose.

The work terminology for this is "urban renewal" – "soft" or "careful"; preserving these contexts represents what the architects at arb mean when they say "ecology." The foundation for this work had to be created politically—as, for example, with above-mentioned laws that Franz Biffiger helped to implement.

Leaving Space for Development: Bern Riding School

It is therefore no surprise that arb, with their social and communicative orientation as an essential component of their professional self-image, confronted the long and arduous preservation and renewal problems of the old riding school in Bern (since 1982).

The riding school project is really a model example of decay, the reevaluation and conversion of historic buildings in the way they presented themselves throughout Europe as a challenging task during the seventies. This task goes

The riding school project is really a model example of decay, the reevaluation and conversion of historic buildings in the way they presented themselves throughout Europe as a challenging task during the seventies. This task goes far beyond the understanding of the preservation of historic buildings valid up to that time (i.e., approximately up to the European year of historic preservation in 1975), which concerned only individual buildings with an approved historic building substance.

far beyond the understanding of the preservation of historic buildings valid up to that time (i.e., approximately up to the European year of historic preservation in 1975), which concerned only individual buildings with an approved historic building substance. Ensemble and quarter, spatial and social contexts moved to the center of attention – the aesthetic and qualitative value of old structures and the economic aspect of their preservation. The young generation had a lot of new uses for abandoned buildings: for making music, theater, dance, meetings in women's, environmental or self-help groups, and many other activities. The book about the relationship between the conversion of abandoned buildings and the independently evolving creativity still needs to be written: empty factory buildings, old mills, useless farms, decaying mining complexes. For Bern, it has already been published and edited by the people running the riding school.

In Bern, the riding school became a magnet for such movements. Like anywhere else, its complex—riding hall, sheds, apartment buildings—were first left to decay by the owner until actors took possession of it and—at first illegally, then tolerated—barely maintained it with their own meager financial resources. The town, as owner, had it patched up at best, but the expert opinion presented by arb upon request revealed that roofs, doors and windows, bathrooms, heat and drainage pipes were damaged or insufficient. Only five years later were first temporary repairs undertaken for partial utilization by the town (autonomous youth center), then a renewal and utilization concept followed which considered the lively activities that had meanwhile settled there. Action groups became partners of the town. Now, in the stables, sheds and apartment houses, there is a restaurant, an event rooms, a print shop and photo lab, movie theater and workshops, women's room and apartment shares; the large hall is open for others to hold events and other activities.

The work by arb is oriented towards preserving and safeguarding this enterprise. For the redevelopment task this means: "careful renewal"—as little interventions as possible, yet effective and lasting. Creating neutral spaces independent from their utilization, spaces that don't predetermine future devel-

36

opments. Proceeding in stages and coordinating the individual steps. The example for this step-by-step renewal that leaves space for future development is the "building shed." The common goal for the utilization is a "covered shared property," which, aside from the permanent institutions, is open to as wide a public as possible—especially the riding hall itself. arb has been committed to this project for 16 years. Its realization has only just begun. The first renovation phase will begin in 1999 with the renovation of the roof and façades, and it's estimated that it will last 3-4 years.

Finesses of a Precious Understatement:
Telecommunications Direction

A totally different aspect of urban renewal is represented by the task that resulted from the conversion and extension of the telecommunications direction (1980–1992) from the fifties in the center of the city. The old and the new buildings had to be connected, along with the administration's extension and apartment houses, a block which, as a street triangle, has to consider the dynamism of the environment. The latter consists of buildings of very different ages and proportions—from 100 year-old gable houses to the extensive horizontal layers of contemporary architecture. arb's architecture replies to this with a subtle unobtrusiveness: additive window slots that excitingly complement the window mass of the old building and react to vertical emphases and proportions in the environment—with the bold fusion of old and new. Or, in this case, also with the discrete, horizontal and vertical geometrically structured coloration of the façade design in which the colors of the quarter are hinted at: a rose-colored gray, a sandy white, a touch of green—yet not in dead plaster but the liveliness of natural limestone.

The representative object cost money—and a lot of time when the building permit was delayed by two years. Finally, the aesthetic passion of an architect could live it up, compulsory but with unrestrained pleasure, when the arb architect in charge, Kurt Aellen, set out on the protracted search. He brought back from French provinces not only the matching limestone for the window para-

pets, panels and vertical strips but also their best wines, whose names he en-joyably lists. Or perhaps it went the other way around: the wine showed him the way to the stones. At any rate, the lava bedrock from the Italian Orvieto has an original creative connection with the wine from there. Thus, the subtle tes-timony of a representative urban renewal came about with the finesse of its precious understatement self-evident in such an unobtrusive way that it looks as if it has long been an integrated component of the city. Again and again, Kurt Aellen draws attention to the subtlety of the details in window profiles, frame reinforcements or reductions; they are specialties of the arb collaborator Lau-rent Cantalou – "our architectural conscience." Other aspects speak for them-selves in an unobtrusive manner when one walks through the buildings: how the old and new building are brought together in the staircase, how skylights expand corridors and rooms, how semi-columns structure and visually short-en the length of the corridors. And how a frosted glass panel at the end of a corridor protects the roof garden of the lower, old house, with the intimacy of the deck chair, the hanging laundry, the cat, from onlookers. Circumspection at its best; it extends to the flower boxes, made of common perforated grid steel in a lightweight framework and the stretched wires for climbing plants, which separate the buffet in the cafeteria from the restaurant tables. "Flower boxes," Aellen quotes the sad experiences of his colleagues, "often cause a lot of spatial ruin later." Here, they're a part of the architecture.

Where do we live? Also in the workplaces, in the public buildings of our towns, in the streets of the city, in the appearance of the houses that catch our eye or tire them. In the wealth of their variety that provides us with elbowroom for life. Our right to "a good place for living" doesn't end at the house or garden door.

SIEDLUNG MERZENACKER

Text Benedikt Loderer   Photos Thomas Keller

DEVELOPMENT MERZENACKER

Seiten 40–49

SIEDLUNG MERZENACKER

*Schon von aussen zeigt sich die
Siedlung als im Ganzen einheitlich,
im Detail jedoch komplex. Der
Widerspruch zwischen individuellen
Wohnbedürfnissen und der
Siedlung als ein architektonisches
Ganzes scheint aufgelöst. Die
Häuser sind untereinander
verschieden und passen doch
zusammen. Eine wichtige Rolle
spielt dabei das Sichtmauerwerk
aus warmgrauem Zementstein.*

Pages 40–49

MERZENACKER DEVELOPMENT

*From the outside, the develop-
ment presents itself as a unified
whole yet complex in its details.
The contradiction between
individual needs and the
development as an architectural
whole seems to be resolved. The
houses vary from one another and
yet they fit together. An important
role is taken on by the exposed
masonry work made of warm
gray hardened cement paste.*

Seiten 50–53

SIEDLUNG MERZENACKER

Die Durchmischung von Wohnen
und Arbeiten belebt die Siedlung.
In diesem Sockelgeschoss sind
Ateliers und ein Kindergarten
untergebracht. Die Stützenreihe der
Arkade bildet eine transparente
Zone zwischen den Arbeitsräumen
und den Gassen und Plätzen.

Seiten 54–59

SIEDLUNG MERZENACKER

Durch die Stahlvorbauten entsteht
eine Raumschicht deren Transparenz mit Storen reguliert werden
kann. Diese Raumschicht ist von
klimatischem und ästhetischem
Nutzen – sie formuliert, bereichert
und verzögert den Übergang von
innen nach aussen in den Garten.

Pages 50-53

DEVELOPMENT MERZENACKER

The combination of living and
working animates the development.
Studios and a kindergarten are
housed in this base story. The
arcade's row of columns forms a
transparent zone between the
workrooms and the alleys and
squares.

Pages 54–59

DEVELOPMENT MERZENACKER

The steel structures in front of the
buildings form a spatial layer
whose transparency can be
regulated via louvered blinds. This
spatial layer functions as a climate
control element and for aesthetics-
it formulates, enriches and delays
the transition from the interior to
the exterior, into the garden.

SIEDLUNG MERZENACKER

*Der mit zenitalem Licht
durchflutete, doppelgeschossige
Innenraum und die offen geführte
Treppe. Hier werden alle wichtigen
Elemente des Hauses zusammengeführt. «Die Steinmauern sind innen
wie aussen speziell für die
Liebkosungen des Streiflichtes
geschaffen worden».*

DEVELOPMENT MERZENACKER

*The two-story interior space
flooded with zenithal light, and the
open staircase. Here, all the
important elements of the house
are brought together. "The stone
walls have been created especially
for the caresses of the sidelight
inside and out."*

Es war ein Ereignis. Der kollektive Mass-anzug gebaut von den Schneidern Ael-len, Cantalou und den andern. Eine De-monstration des Zwischenraums. Zwi-schen den Häusern entsteht er und ist beides: Verlängerung des Innenraums und Anteil am allgemeinen Aussenraum. Früher sprachen wir von Hof, Gasse und Platz. Dieses Formenvokabular hat arb in einer zeitgenössischen Form weiter-geführt. Doch eigentlich sind es alte Re-zepte. Entscheide dich für private oder öffentliche Nutzung, heisst die erste Re-gel. Ziehe deutliche Grenzen. Mach die private wirklich privat, die öffentliche wirklich öffentlich. Trotzdem, sagt die zweite Regel, vermittle zwischen den bei-den Nutzungen. Beim Eingang zuerst, der ein Übergang sein soll. Da, wo du deinen Nachbarn begegnest, wo du dein Velo-gerümpel verstaust, wo deine Gäste an-kommen. Da auch, wo du dein Hausge-sicht zeigst. Nütze für diesen Übergang die Höhendifferenzen. Genauer: diffe-renziere in der Höhe. Denke im Schnitt. Dann mache eine Zwischenschicht gegen den Garten, baue ein Glashaus ein. Dif-ferenziere nicht bloss in der Höhe, son-dern auch im Klima.

Diese beiden Regeln, die sich wider-sprechen, gilt es auszugleichen. Es ist die Paul-Hofer-Predigt. Der sich verschränk-ende Stadtraum, die Hierarchie der öf-fentlichen Räume, das, was Hofer in Böh-men, der Toskana, in Noto und auch in Thun längst gefunden und allen vorge-führt hat. Ex negativo ausgedrückt: Ver-biete dir jedes Abstandsgrün. Bleib spe-

It was an event. The collective, custom-made suit by the tailors Aellen, Cantalou and others. A demonstration of the in-terstitial space. It emerges between the houses and is both an extension of the interior and part of the common exterior space. Earlier, we spoke of yard, alley and square. This formal vocabulary was continued by arb in a contemporary form. But in reality they are old recipes. The first rule is to decide on private or pub-lic use. Draw clear borders. Make the pri-vate truly private, the public truly public. And yet, says the second rule, mediate between the two uses. First, at the en-trance, which should be a transition. There, where you meet your neighbors, where you put away your bicycle stuff, where your guests arrive, and where you show the face of your house. Use the dif-ferences in height for this transition. More precisely: differentiate in height. Think in sections. Then add an intersti-tial layer towards the garden; build in a glass house. Don't just differentiate in height, but also in climate.

The task is to balance these two contra-dictory rules. It's the Paul Hofer sermon. The crossing urban space, the hierarchy of public spaces, that which Hofer had long ago discovered and revealed to everyone in Bohemia, Tuscany, Noto and Thun. Expressed ex negative: do not al-low yourself any distance-giving green-ery. Remain special, don't do anything commonplace.

Commonplace should be only the house type, the row house. And the architec-

ziell, mach nichts Allgemeines. Allgemein sei nur der Haustyp, das Reihenhaus. Und die architektonische Sprache. Zementstein, Glas und Stahl. Damit binde das Auseinanderstrebende zusammen. Abbé Laugiers Losung «de l'unité dans le détail et du tumulte dans l'ensemble». Ein Satz aus dem 18. Jahrhundert, der auch dem jungen Le Corbusier gefallen hat, als er ihn 1915 in der Bibliothèque Nationale las.

Das Kapitel Merzenacker hat noch eine Fortsetzung. Sie heisst Licht. Genauer: Lichtführung. Licht, nicht Beleuchtung. In der Architektur gibt es nur ein Licht, das des Himmels. Mit ihm umgehen, heisst Architektur machen. An ihrer Lichtführung werdet ihr sie erkennen. Im Merzenacker – der hier die Stellvertretung für die andern arb-Bauten übernimmt – ist die Lichtführung vorgeführt. Licht braucht Entfaltungsmöglichkeit, was mit Raum, sogar Raumhöhe übersetzt werden muss. Darum die zweigeschossigen Räume mit Oberlichtern, die Herzen der Häuser. Das Zenitallicht ist das wahre, das Architektenlicht.
Dann braucht es auch eine Wand, worauf das Licht seine Schattenzeichnungen werfen kann. Die Steinmauern sind innen wie aussen speziell für die Liebkosungen des Streiflichts geschaffen worden. Ihr Fugenbild zeichnet auch in die Schwärze des Schattens eine Schraffur und wirft ein Ordnungsnetz über die graue Fläche. An den Fassaden schneiden späte Nachfahren der Lisenen Schat-

tural language. Hardened cement paste, glass and steel. With them, tie together what wants to move apart. Abbé Laugier's motto "de l'unité dans le détail et du tumulte dans l'ensemble" (unity in the details and tumult in the ensemble). A sentence from the 18th century that also pleased young Le Corbusier when he read it in the Bibilothèque Nationale in 1915.

The Merzenacker chapter does have a continuation. It is called light. More precisely: the guiding of the light. Light, not lighting. In architecture, there is only one light. From the sky. Dealing with it means making architecture. You shall recognize them by how they guide the light. In the Merzenacker—taking on the representation of the other arb buildings here— the guidance of the light is being demonstrated. Light needs the possibility to unfold, which has to be translated with space, and even spatial height. Hence the two-story rooms with skylights, the hearts of the houses. The zenithal light is the true light, the architect's light.
Then it takes a wall onto which the light can throw its shadow drawings. The stone walls, inside and outside, were created especially to receive the caresses of the sidelight. The image of their joints etches a crosshatched pattern into the blackness of the shadow, covering the gray surface with a structural web. Late descendents of the lesenes cut shadow edges, field divisions and proportional rectangles out of the surfaces on the facades, and the horizontal steel supports

tenkanten, Feldereinteilungen, Proportionsrechtecke aus den Flächen, und die waagrechten Stahlträger darunter unterstreichen mit einem Schattenquerstrich die Geschossunterteilung. Ob sich diese «klassischen», ruhigen Flächen still gegen den Tumult des Gestänges der Terrassen und Wintergärten auflehnen?

Zum Merzenacker macht Kurt Aellen noch einen wichtigen Nachtrag. Er habe das Grundstück selber geschneidert. Dabei ging er von einer Verzahnung ins bestehende Quartier aus. Er wollte keine Insel der Seligen, sondern einen Bestandteil der Stadt. Es war auch eine Erweiterung durch andere Architekten vorgesehen. Die Weg-Führung sollte die Nachbarn durch die Siedlung lotsen. Eingehen auf den Ort und Schaffen eines Ortes sind hier dasselbe.

below underline the division of the stories with a shadow line. Might these "classical" calm surfaces quietly revolt against the tumult of the rods on the terraces and solariums?

Kurt Aellen makes an important addendum to the Merzenacker. He himself has tailored the site. In doing so, he presumed an interlocking with the existing quarter. He wasn't trying to achieve an island of the blessed but rather an integrated component of the town. An extension by other architects was also planned. The course of the pathways was to guide the neighbors through the development. Responding to the site and creating a site are the same here.

SITUATION   SITE PLAN

MERZENACKER

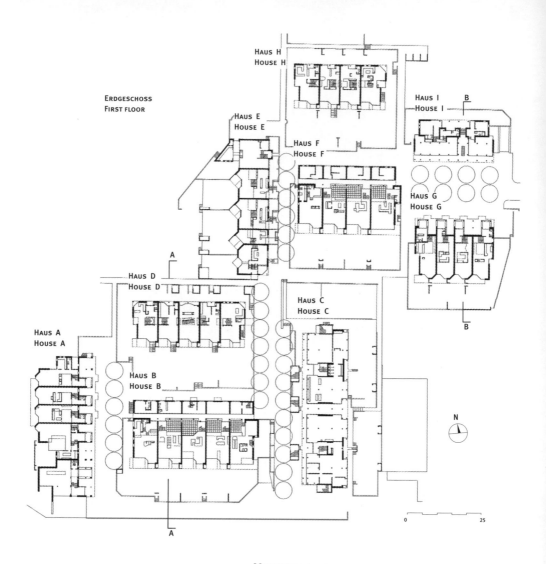

ERDGESCHOSS
FIRST FLOOR

HAUS H
HOUSE H

HAUS I   B
HOUSE I

HAUS E
HOUSE E

HAUS F
HOUSE F

HAUS G
HOUSE G

A

HAUS D
HOUSE D

HAUS C
HOUSE C

HAUS A
HOUSE A

HAUS B
HOUSE B

B

N

A

0   25

MERZENACKER

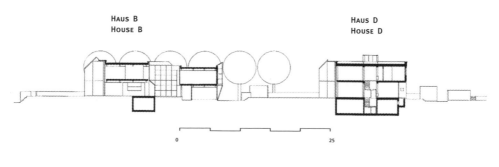

HAUS B
HOUSE B

HAUS D
HOUSE D

0   25

SCHNITT A – A   SECTION A – A

74

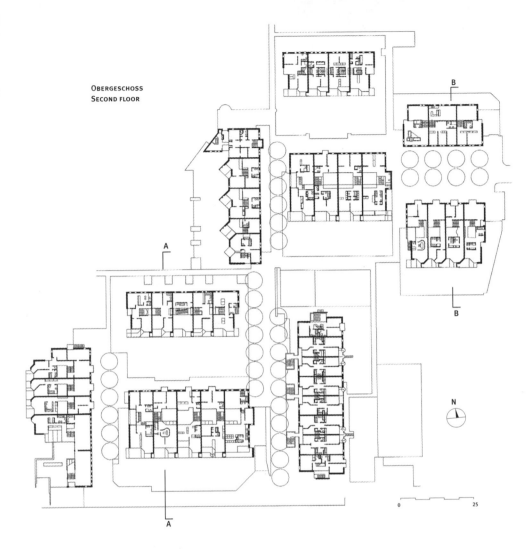

B

A

A

B

B

N

0   25

MERZENACKER

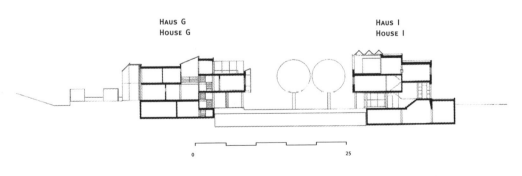

HAUS G
HOUSE G

HAUS I
HOUSE I

0   25

SCHNITT B – B   SECTION B – B

KONZENTRIERT
KONZEPTUELL
KONSTRUKTIV

Text Benedikt Loderer

Photos Leonardo Bezzola (Freies Gymnasium), Balthasar Burkhard (Ulmizberg)

CONCENTRATED
CONCEPTUAL
CONSTRUCTIVE

Zwei Bauten von arb waren für Architekturstudenten damals obligatorisch: Freies Gymnasium (1966–72) und der Turm auf dem Ulmizberg (1970–75). Der «Freigymer», das war neu. Das grosse Rechteck mit den Löchern. Ein Gebäude, das nicht Funktionen aneinanderreihte, nichts da von Pavillon oder andern ablesbaren Deutlichkeiten, hier herrschte ein anderes Prinzip: Die Schachtel mit Auskerbungen. Corbu hat dieses schon in «Vers une Architecture» gezeichnet und mit «très difficile» unterstrichen. Hallers strahlende Kästen oder Schaders Freudenberg sind uneheliche Verwandte. Nur: Beim Freigymer sprachen die Architekten einen technischen Dialekt. Das war nicht mehr gebaut, sondern montiert. Der Architekturstudent stand da und wollte werden wie arb: konzentriert, konzeptuell, konstruktiv. Architektur ist eine Metallkonstruktion.

Ein Name von besonderem Glanz ist mit dem Sendeturm auf dem Ulmizberg verknüpft: Jean Prouvé. Zur Frankreichorientierung von arb gehört auch er. In Zürich war Prouvé ein Name, ein Gegenstand der Ausstellung, aber sicher kein Mann, mit dem man zusammenarbeitet. Für unlösbare Fälle geht man dort zu Ove Arup nach London. Prouvé auf dem Ulmizberg. Er wird als Konstrukteur wahrgenommen. Für die Fassade eingesetzt. Er muss auf die jungen Leute von damals einen grossen Eindruck gemacht haben. Diese unschweizerische Kombinierer-Mentalität, die aus allem etwas machen

Two buildings by arb were obligatory back then for the students of architecture: the grammar school (1966–72) and the tower on Ulmizberg (1970–75). The "Freies Gymnasium." That was new. The large rectangle with the holes. A building that didn't line up functions, no noticeable pavilion or any other perceivable clarity. A different principle ruled here: the box with notches. Le Corbusier had already drawn it in "Vers une Architecture" and emphasized it with "très difficile." Haller's radiating boxes or Schader's Freudenberg are illegitimate relatives. But: in the case of the "Freies Gymnasium," the architects spoke a technical dialect. This was no longer built; it was assembled. The architectural student just stood there and wanted to become like arb: concentrated, conceptual, constructive. Architecture is a metal construction.

A name of special distinction is connected with the radio tower on Ulmizberg: Jean Prouvé. He is also part of arb's orientation towards France. In Zurich, Prouvé was a name, an subject of the exhibition, but certainly not a man with whom one would collaborate. For unsolvable cases, one goes to Ove Arup in London. Prouvé on Ulmizberg. He is perceived as a constructor. Used for the façade. He must have made a big impression on the young people back then. This un-Swiss mentality of combining that can make something out of almost anything. Building with semi-prefabricated products, seeing more possibilities in the objects

77

kann. Das Bauen mit Halbfertigfabrikaten, in den Gegenständen mehr Möglichkeiten sehen, als ihre Erfinder sich je haben vorstellen können. Das Haus von Charles und Ray Eames in Santa Monica, zusammengesetzt aus dem Katalog, war auch so ein Fixpunkt der Betrachtung. Es war eine Befreiung von der Baufachkunde System von Lerber und Hess, von all diesen Leuten, die mit einer Sechskantschraube nichts anzufangen wussten.

Das Leichte ist besser als das Schwere, das Gefügte klüger als das Massive, das Flexible dem Starren überlegen. Wovon die Modernen aus der Zwischenkriegszeit nur geredet hatten, jetzt war es möglich: das geschraubte Haus. Auf dem Ulmizberg steht ein geschraubter Turm. Dass er mit Corten eingefasst ist, gehört zur Zeitstimmung. Die Schönheit des Rostes musste erst entdeckt und gegen den Travertin durchgesetzt werden. Luginbühls Plastiken protzten geradezu mit dem ungewaschenen Rost. In ihm steckt Natursehnsucht, das Eisen begegnet dem Wetter. Das Ungeputzte fasziniert. Leider war der Rost stärker als das Blech und frass es durch. Künstlerpech. Als der Turm renoviert wurde, war er eingerüstet. Und plötzlich hatte er eine neue Dimension. Er stand an der Bergkante nicht mehr als eine von filigranen Stäben umhüllte, gestufte, aufgestützte Masse, sondern als massiver, übergrosser Klotz, unförmig und urtümlich. Er war plötzlich so gross wie das Fernsehzeitalter geworden.

than their inventors could ever dream of. The house by Charles and Ray Eames in Santa Monica, assembled from the catalog, was one such fixed point of reflection. It was liberation from the architectural science system by Lerber and Hess, from all these people who didn't know what to do with a square-head bolt.

The light is better than the weighty, the assembled smarter than the massive, the flexible superior to the rigid. What the Modernists had only talked about in the time between the wars was now possible: the screwed-together house. On Ulmizberg stands a screwed-together tower. The fact that it is surrounded by Corten steel is part of the zeitgeist. The beauty of rust first had to be discovered and needed to prevail against Travertine. Luginbühl's sculptures literally showed off with the unwashed rust. A desire for nature is hidden in it; the iron meets the weather. The un-cleaned is fascinating. Unfortunately, the rust was stronger than the sheet metal and ate through it. Too bad. When the tower was renovated, it was surrounded by scaffolds. And suddenly, it had a new dimension. It stood at the edge of the mountain no longer as a shelled volume, stepped and supported by filigree rods, but as a massive, oversized block, bulky and archaic. Suddenly, it had become as big as the age of television.

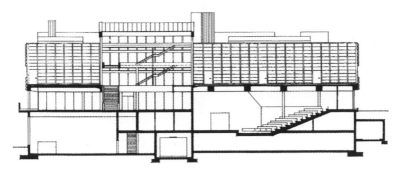

QUERSCHNITT: BIOLOGIEGARTEN – HALLE – PAUSENHOF/SAAL
CROSS SECTION: BIOLOGY GARDEN – LOBBY – SCHOOLYARD/HALL

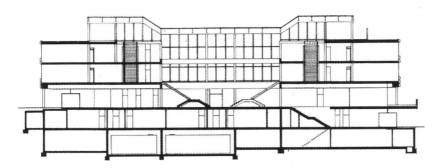

LÄNGSSCHNITT: SCHULRÄUME – HALLE – SCHULRÄUME
LONGITUDINAL SECTION: CLASSROOMS – LOBBY – CLASSROOMS

0   25

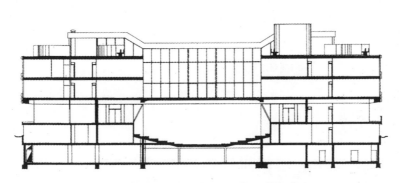

LÄNGSSCHNITT: SCHULRÄUME – PAUSENHOF/SAAL – SCHULRÄUME
LONGITUDINAL SECTION: SCHOOLYARD/HALL – CLASSROOMS

FREIES GYMNASIUM BERN

Seiten 80/81
FREIES GYMNASIUM BERN
*Die Anlage ist rechteckig, nahezu
quadratisch, und von einer
Aluminium-Vorhangfassade ganz
umschlossen. Auch die
Aussenräume liegen innen.*

Seiten 82/83
FREIES GYMNASIUM BERN
*Von der Halle aus werden alle
Räume erschlossen. Die
Klassenzimmer, die Aula, die
Turnhallen und die innenliegenden
Aussenräume: der Pausenhof,
der Biologiegarten und die
Pausenplätze auf dem Dach.*

Seiten 84/85
FREIES GYMNASIUM BERN
*Blick auf den Pausenhof und in die
zentrale Halle. Auf dem Dach über
den Klassenzimmern liegt einer der
beiden räumlich reich gestalteten
Pausenplätze.*

Seiten 88–95
ULMIZBERG
*Der Turm steht an der Hangkante
mitten im Wald. Anstelle von Beton
(Wettbewerbsvorgabe) wählte arb
eine transparente windsteife Stahlkonstruktion, die sich natürlicher
in die Waldsilhouette integriert.
Der weltweit erste Richtstrahl-
antennen-Träger aus Stahl ist das
Resultat einer intensiven Auseinandersetzung mit dem Ort.*

Pages 80/81
FREIES GYMNASIUM BERN
*The grammar school complex is
rectangular, almost square, and
completely surrounded by an
aluminum curtain façade.
The outdoor rooms are also inside.*

Pages 82/83
FREIES GYMNASIUM BERN
*All rooms are accessible via the
lobby. The classrooms, the aula,
the gymnasiums and the inside/
outdoor rooms: the schoolyard,
the biology garden and the
schoolyards on the roof.*

Pages 84/85
FREIES GYMNASIUM BERN
*View of the schoolyard and the
central lobby. One of the two richly
spatial schoolyards is located on
the roof above the classrooms.*

Pages 88–95
ULMIZBERG
*The tower is situated on a slope in
the middle of a forest. Instead of
concrete (competition stipulation)
arb chose a transparent, wind-
braced steel construction that
naturally integrates into the
silhouette of the forest. The first
directional antennae tower in the
world made of steel is the result
of an intense confrontation
with the site.*

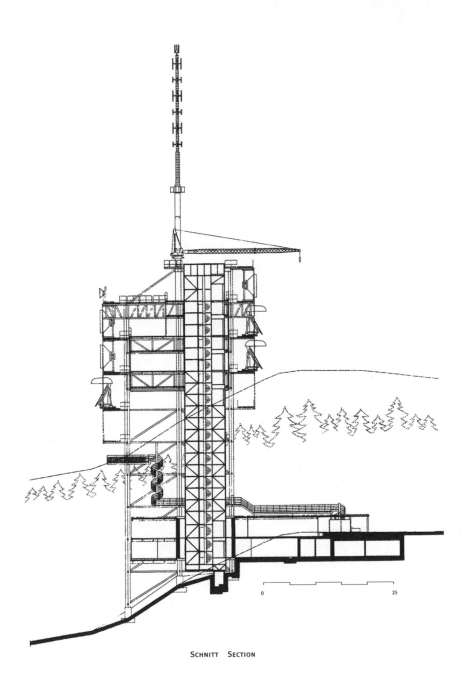

SCHNITT SECTION

ULMIZBERG

*Der Ort, die Frage der Angemessenheit
und das scheinbar Selbstverständliche
der Interventionen stehen im
Vordergrund von Dominique Uldrys
Photo-Essay.*

*The location, the question of suitability
and the seemingly self-evident nature
of the interventions are in the fore-
ground of Dominique Uldry's photo
essays.*

CONTEXT

Photos Dominique Uldry   Text Benedikt Loderer

HAUS BRUNNADERN

Ein Restgrundstück im Brunnadernquartier. Der Baumeister Ghielmetti hatte da noch einen Schuppen, der als Garage diente. Gegenüber steht das landwirtschaftlich anmutende Gebäude, worin das Büro arb seit Jahren sitzt und welches es auch selbst umgebaut hat. Es hat den Charme des Unfertigen, Unaufgeräumten, Provisorischen. Hier wird gearbeitet, nicht repräsentiert. In der Ecke ein Wohnhaus aus der Zwischenkriegszeit, von arb mit einem Anbau erweitert. Hier auf dem Ghielmetti-Gelände hat arb in den 30 Jahren sein Biotop besetzt, ausgebaut und erweitert. Es sind die baulichen Zeugen einer Bürogeschichte, ein Ensemble baut sein Ensemble.

Und jetzt an Stelle der Garage neu ein Wohn- und Geschäftshaus. arb ist diesmal Bauherrschaft und Architekt zugleich. Mischung auch hier. Über einem hohen Sockel mit Büros für einen Bauingenieur und ein chinesisches Erlöstwerdezentrum drei Wohngeschosse. Im runden Kopf noch eine Wohnung mit Stöckli. Die Nutzungsteilung wird dargestellt, vor allem auf der Eingangsseite, wo geschosshohe Säulen die horizontale Schichtung betonen. Wiederum eine Schnittlösung, diesmal längsgeteilt. Auf der Eingangsseite ein direkt belichtetes anderthalbhohes Kellergeschoss und darüber im Hochparterre eine normalhohe Schicht. Auf der Gartenseite die umgekehrte Reihenfolge: Im Untergeschoss Normalhöhe, darüber auf Hofniveau der Anderthalbgeschosser. Tiefe

HOUSE BRUNNADERN

Brunnadern quarter: a leftover piece of property. The contractor Ghielmetti used to have a shed there that served as a garage. Across from it is the building with an agricultural appearance that was converted by arb; the office has had its headquarters in it for years. The charm of the unfinished, unorganized and provisional building serves the work that takes place inside; its not representative of the company. In the corner, an apartment house from the time between the wars, extended by arb with an addition. Here on the Ghielmetti property, arb has claimed, developed and extended its biotope over the course of 30 years. These are the architectural witnesses of an office history; an ensemble is building an ensemble.

And now, instead of the garage, there is a new building for residential and commercial use. This time, arb is both client and architect. And there is mixture here, as well. Above a high base, which accommodates offices for a building engineer and a Chinese redemption center, there are three residential levels. In the rounded head of the building, an additional apartment and studio. The shared use is revealed above all on the entrance side, where floor-to-ceiling columns enhance the horizontal layering. Again, a sectional solution is divided lengthwise in this case. On the entrance side we find a directly lit, one-and-a-half-floor-high basement level, and above it, a layer of normal height on the mezzanine. The se-

Wohnungsgrundrisse, verglaste Balkone, wieder wird das Thema Wohnwert durchbuchstabiert. Aellen, Cantalou und Thomas Keller haben sich hier eingenistet und jeder hat seine Wohnung sehr persönlich besetzt, von Teakholz-Abdeckungen bis Leerstehenlassen kann das gehen.

Die Rundung gibt dem Gebäude eine Richtung und ruft in Architekten das Bild «Schiff» hervor. Eine rettende Arche, der Aufbruch an neue Ufer, ein technisches Wunderwerk? Kaum, es ist ein behäbiges, werkbares Linienschiff der Anständigen Rationalen Bauvernunft (ARB). Das geht so schnell nicht unter.

SCHULHEIM SCHLOSS ERLACH

Auf einem Politausflug, erzählt Franz Biffiger, habe ihm einer der Grossräte gesagt, man merke gar nicht, dass da etwas neu ist. Gemeint war das Schulheim Schloss Erlach. Der Wettbewerb lief bereits 1975, und die Ausführung war rund zehn Jahre (!) später beendet. In dieser Zeit wurde die Denkmalpflege erfunden, jedenfalls ihre politische Macht. 1975 war das Europäische Denkmalpflegejahr, und ein neuer Begriff machte Karriere: die historische Substanz. Von den bestehenden Bauten zur historischen Substanz ist ein gewaltiger Veredelungsschritt. Das Alte wird wertvoll als Zeitzeuge (auch ein neues Wort), es braucht den Adelstitel der kunstgeschichtlichen Bedeutungsweihe längst nicht mehr, das bürgerliche Nochvorhandensein genügt. Das Schloss und das Städtchen Erlach

quence is reversed on the garden side: normal height for the basement floor, above it, on the level of the yard, the one-and-a-half-floor layer. Deep apartment plans, glazed balconies: again, the theme of residential value is spelled out. Aellen, Cantalou and Thomas Keller have made their "nest" here, and each one has occupied his apartment in a very personal way – from teak wood paneling to simply letting it sit empty.

The rounded building head provides the structure with a direction and evokes the image "ship!" among architects. An ark, a journey towards new shores, a technical marvel? Hardly so. It is a portly, functional, scheduled ship listening to the reason of Anständige Rationale Bauvernunft (ARB), and it won't easily sink.

SCHOOL HOSTEL ERLACH CASTLE

On a political excursion, Franz Biffinger recounts, one of the canton councilors told him that it wasn't obvious that there was something new. He meant the school hostel in Erlach Castle. The competition took place back in 1975, and the execution was finished about ten years later. During this time, the preservation of historic buildings and monuments was invented, or at least its political power. 1975 was the year of European historic preservation, and a new term made its debut: the "historic substance." It's a tremendous step of refinement to get from the existing buildings to the historic substance. The old becomes precious as a "witness of time" (also a new term),

sind eigentlich unantastbar. Der Landvogt haust immer noch unsichtbar in seinen Mauern. arb stapelt darum tief, unterzieht sich, tritt leise auf und passt sich ein. Hier herrscht nicht die Entweder-oder-Haltung vor, die will, dass das Alte vom Neuen scharf abgesetzt werde, das was Campi-Pessina-Piazzoli mit dem Museo Castello Montebello in Bellinzona vorgeführt haben. Für arb gibt es diese rechthaberische Trennlinie nicht. Sie operieren weniger grundsätzlich, geben sich versöhnlich. Jedes Erlach ist speziell, ein Sonderfall, mit Glaubenssätzen allein wird man ihm nicht gerecht.

Ein neues Gebot der Denkmalpflege wird hier erfüllt: Die Brandmauern sind heilig. Wer die Altstadt erhalten will, muss ihre Parzellenstruktur bewahren. Die vier Altstadthäuser, die die Wohngruppen aufnehmen, werden als unabhängige Einheiten belassen, und der Zwischenbau fügt sich in eine Baulücke, als hätte hier schon immer ein solches Haus gestanden. Der Grossrat jedenfalls hat nichts gemerkt. Es gibt auch in der Architektur Bescheidenheit.

Biffiger dazu: «Trotz dieser Bescheidenheit haben wir Wirkung erzielt: Das durch die Struktur der Bausubstanz inspirierte, neue Heimmodell wurde anschliessend vom Kanton Bern für andere Heime übernommen.»

and it is way beyond needing the noble title of the art-historic consecration of importance. The civil fact of still existing is enough.

The castle and the town of Erlach are really sacrosanct. The landvogt still lives unseen behind his ramparts. arb therefore understate, submit themselves, act quietly and adapt. The either/or attitude doesn't reign here, wanting the old to be clearly distinct from the new, which Campi-Pessina-Piazzoli have demonstrated with the Museo Castello Montebello in Bellinzona. For arb, this dogmatic separation line doesn't exist. They operate less fundamentally, present themselves in a conciliatory manner. Every Erlach is special, a special case, and one can not do them justice with tenets alone.

Here, a new law of historic preservation is fulfilled: the firewalls are sacrosanct. Those who want to preserve the old part of town have to preserve its parcel structure. The four old town buildings that house the groups are left untouched as independent units, and the interim building fills a gap as though such a house had always been standing there. The councilor, at least, didn't notice anything. There still is modesty in architecture, too.

Biffiger says: "Despite this modesty, we have achieved an effect: the new hostel model inspired by the structure of the building substance was later adapted by the canton of Bern for other hostels."

FERNMELDEDIREKTION BERN

Fernmeldedirektion (1980–92). Eigentlich ist Walter Schwaars Bürohaus von 1952 mit seinen Rasterfassaden à la Salvisberg gar nicht so schlecht. Aber es brauchte 30 Jahre, bis unsereiner das zugeben konnte. Dieses Gebäude und das Wohnhaus diagonal gegenüber bilden die Ecken eines verzogenen Vierecks, in das hinein die Neubauten einzufügen waren. Da wo der Verkehr (damals) am geringsten war, stellte arb die Wohnzeile hin. Die neuen Bürogebäude schliessen den Block, allerdings unvollständig. Im Innern steht die Aula auf Stützen, ein früherer Weg ist als Durchgang noch zu spüren.

Die Stichworte heissen Ensemble und Stadtreparatur. Der Blockrand wurde in den achtziger Jahren wiederentdeckt. Doch hier wird nicht nach einer geschlossenen Figur gesucht. Jedes Gebäude zeigt seine Funktion an, und gemeinsam bilden sie eine vielfältige Einheit. Ein gewordenes Konglomerat wird zum gewollten. Klar dominierend ist Schwaars Ecke. Sie gibt dem Ensemble die Richtung zum Eigerplatz hin. Die Neubauten sind daran herangeschoben. Die Wohnzeile nimmt sich trotz ihrer etwas gar bewegten Fassade noch mehr zurück. Und überraschend sind es Natursteinfassaden. Dünne Platten vor viel Isolation, wie das Gesetz es befahl. Ich wundere mich. Nach dem Meccano, dem Rostblech, den unverputzten Zementsteinen, nun Naturstein. Gewiss, es ist ein innerstädtischer Standort, trotzdem. Gibt es ein arb-typi-

TELECOMMUNICATION DIRECTION BERN

Telecommunication Direction (1980–92). Walter Schwaar's office building, which dates back to 1952, with its grid-like façades à la Salvisberg, isn't that bad after all. But it took thirty years until someone like myself could admit it. This building and the apartment house standing diagonally across from it form the corners of a distorted square into which the new buildings had to be placed. Where (back then) there used to be the lightest traffic, arb placed the row of houses. The new office buildings terminate the block, although incompletely. Inside, the aula rests on supports and the echo of a former pathway can still be perceived in a passageway.

The keywords are ensemble and urban renewal. The block edge was rediscovered during the eighties. But in this case, an enclosed form is not the goal. Each building indicates its function, and together they form a divers unity. An evolved conglomerate becomes a desired one. Schwaar's corner is clearly dominating. It provides the ensemble with an orientation towards Eigerplatz. The new buildings are pushed towards it. The housing row, despite its rather lively façade, withdraws even more. And, surprisingly, these are natural stone façades. Thin panels in front of insulation, as required by the regulations. I wonder... After the Meccano—the rusted sheets, the barefaced concrete blocks—it's natural stone now. Sure, it's an inner city location, but still... Is there a material typ-

sches Material? Keines gefunden. arb hat sich nie über ein bestimmtes Material definiert, es gibt keine vorgefassten Entschlüsse, wie etwas umzusetzen sei. Die Materialwahl variiert von Fall zu Fall. Konsequent innerhalb einer Aufgabe, das immer, doch nie der hochgezüchtete Markenartikel. Zu arb fallen mir keine fertigen Bilder ein.

Atriumhäuser Kalchacker

Das Reizwort heisst Baufeld. Ein baurechtlich und geometrisch desinfiziertes Terrain, bereit zur Operation. Nur hier, nur dies, aber soviel, steht in der Gebrauchsanweisung der Überbauung Kalchacker in Bremgarten. Die übrigen Baufelder sind bereits gefüllt, mit sittlich-ländlichem Giebeltanz, jetzt muss arb Stand gewinnen. Sie nehmen ein Thema auf, das seit Aumatt immer schon da war und im Merzenacker bereits einmal durchgespielt wurde: die grosse Bautiefe mit innerer Lichtquelle. Doch sind es diesmal Geschosswohnungen, die selbstverständlich Planungsflexibilität erlauben müssen. 24 Meter von Fassade zu Fassade! Die Lösung heisst Innenhof, Lichthof, ein Sodbrunnen fürs Tageslicht. Hof und Treppenhaus stanzen Löcher in die tiefen, schmalen Grundrisse. Doch die Wohnungen bleiben durchgehend, in der Mitte kerbt sie der Lichthof ein. Es entstehen Durchblicke von über zwanzig Metern zur Freude der Leute, die in den Stüblis nicht leben können und wenigstens an einer Stelle Grosszügigkeit und nicht bloss Wohn-

ical for arb? Haven't found one yet. arb never defined themselves through a specific material; there are no predetermined decisions on how to realize something. The choice of material is determined on a case to case basis – always consequential within a specific task, but never the fancy brand article. I can't come up with any complete image with respect to arb.

Atrium Houses Kalchacker

The emotive word is: building zone. A disinfected terrain with respect to building laws and geometry, ready for operation. Only here, only this, but this much is written in the operating manual of the Kalchacker development in Bremgarten. The remaining sites are already filled with a moral-rural gable dance, and now arb has to gain its own status. They pick up a theme that has been around since Aumatt and has already been played through once in Merzenacker: a large building depth with an inner source of light. But this time we are dealing with apartment units that naturally have to allow for flexibility in planning. 24 meters from façade to façade! The solution is called inner courtyard, light yard, a well for daylight. Yard and staircase punch holes into the deep, narrow ground plan. But the apartments remain intact. In the middle of the structure, the light yard creates notches in the ground plan. Outlooks of twenty meters are the result, pleasing the people who find it difficult to live in small rooms and need a more generous amount of space, and not just

fläche brauchen. Gegen Westen eine tiefe, vor das Gebäude gestellte Balkonschicht, leb- und belebbar. Konsequente Ost-Westorientierung mit Südkopf, eigentlich fast aus dem Lehrbuch. Das Konzept folgt aber nicht der Hoftypologie, sondern ist aus einem Schottendenken entwickelt. Dass die Wohnungen durchgehend sind, das ist das Entscheidende. Das Thema heisst: Die Überwindung der Bautiefe. Der Gebrauch der Innenhöfe wird dabei besonders interessieren. Wird die Abschirmung oder der Austausch überwiegen?

Warum die Tonnendächer? Ein verlorenes Gefecht im Flachdachkrieg, das kleinere Übel in einer Gemeinde, wo das Wort «Dorf» zur Befestigung des Eigenmietwertes dient. Allerdings tun die Tonnendächer so, als ob darunter Reihenhäuser wären und nicht Geschosswohnungen mit Wohnungstrennwänden, die sich um die «Hauseinteilung» überhaupt nicht kümmern.

Behindertenheim La Pimpinière

Nach Malleray am selben Samstag noch. Von Bern nach Biel hat man die Tatsachen vor dem Autofenster: Die Schweiz ist schön. Grün und zersiedelt. Hinter Biel die Schweiz der Kunstbauten. Über der Taubenlochschlucht kreuzen sich die Brücken der verschiedenen Generationen. Hierzulande wird Sience Fiction gebaut, immer vorausgesetzt, dass es sich um Verkehrsbauten handelt. Malleray, wo liegt das? Hinten rechts, im Tal einer grünen Bergwelle. Am Hang darüber ein Pa-

apartment space, at least in one area. Towards the west, a deep layer of balconies, which can also function as living space, is placed in front of the building. Almost a textbook, consequential east-west orientation with a southern head. The concept, however, does not follow the yard typology but has been developed from a concept of sealing off. What's decisive is that the apartments cover the floor space. The theme is to overcome the building depth. The use of the inner courtyards will be of special interest. What will prevail: the screening or the exchange?

Why the barrel vaulted roofs? A lost battle in the flat roof war, the lesser evil in a community where the word "village" serves to fortify proper rental values. And yet, the vaulted roofs act as though row houses were beneath them and not apartment units with separating walls that don't care about the "house division."

Home for the Handicapped
La Pimpinière

After Malleray. From Bern to Biel, the evidence is right outside the car window: Switzerland is beautiful. Green and spoiled by uncontrolled development. After Biel, the Switzerland of the man-made constructions. Above the Taubenloch gorge the bridges from the different generations cross. Science Fiction is built here, always under the precondition that we're dealing with transportation structures. Malleray? Where's that? Back to the right, in the valley of a green mountain

lazzo. Früher standen die Herrenhäuser so über den Dörfern, heute ist es ein Heim für Schwerstbehinderte.

Das Stichwort Palazzo bestätigt sich, wenn man aus dem Auto steigt. Von einem Säulengang eingefasster Hof, zinoberroter Putz, arb überrascht mit einem Stück Italianità auf tausend Meter Jurahöhe. Neue Leute am Werk? Es sind kaum mehr die Rossischüler, sondern eher Campis Kinder, die viel Siza studiert haben. Hier herrscht die selbstverständliche Eleganz, die sich mit dem mediterranen Architektenalphabet buchstabiert. Der Hof, die Halle, die Säule, der Belvedere-Balkon, das Gesimse, die Einfassung, der Sockel, zusammenfassend: das gemauerte Haus.

Ein Palazzo für Schwerstbehinderte. Wir werden herumgeführt. Jede Tür ist eine Barriere, die Schlüsselgewalt der Erzieherin belehrt uns, dass hier eine geschlossene, überwachte Gesellschaft wohnt, ein Sonderfall des menschlichen Zusammenlebens. Alles ist hell und freundlich, aber trotzdem bedrückend. Die aus dem Schloss gerissene Zimmertüre erinnert an Gewaltanwendung. Dieser Palazzo ist auch ein Gehege. Nur die Hälfte der Bewohner läuft frei herum.

Die Cafeteria mit klugem Querschnitt und Blick über Dorf und Land. Das gegenüberliegende Tannengrün hat etwas Melancholisches, wie der Bau auch. Die offizielle Heiterkeit kontrastiert mit der tatsächlichen Schwerstbehinderung. Manchmal ist auch die Architektur ratlos.

wave. On the slope above it, a palazzo. In the old days, the mansions were placed like that above the village; today it serves as a home for the severely handicapped. Palazzo, the headword, is confirmed when getting out of the car. A yard surrounded by a colonnade, vermilion plaster, arb surprises us with a piece of Italianità a thousand meters high in the Jurassic Alps. New people at work? They're hardly the Rossi students; rather, they are Campi's children, who have studied a lot of Siza. The self-understood elegance that is spelled out with the Mediterranean architectural alphabet prevails here. The yard, the hall, the column, the belvedere balcony, the cornice, the frames, and the base – in brief: the masonry house.

A palazzo for severely handicapped people. We're getting the tour. Each door is a barrier; the authority of the nurse teaches us that a closed, monitored society resides here, a special case in human coexistence. Everything is bright and friendly and yet rather depressing. The door ripped out of the lock indicates the use of violent force. This palazzo is also an enclosure. Only half the inhabitants are allowed to walk around freely. The cafeteria has a clever cross-section and view of the village and landscape. The green of the pines on the other side has something of a melancholic quality, like the building itself. The official cheerfulness contrasts with the factual handicap. Sometimes, architecture is also handicapped.

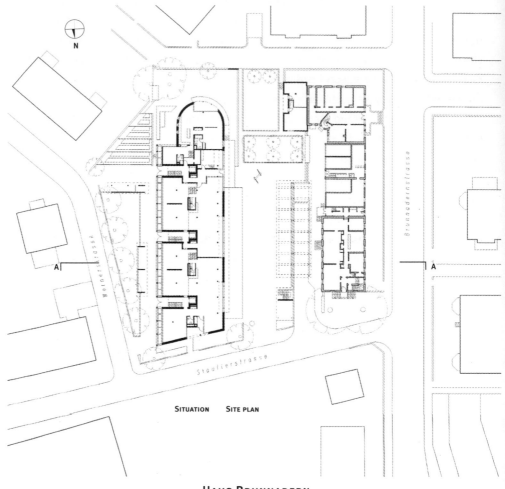

SITUATION   SITE PLAN

HAUS BRUNNADERN
HOUSE BRUNNADERN

0   25

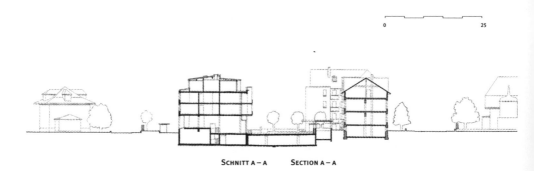

SCHNITT A – A   SECTION A – A

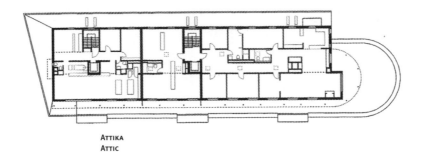

ATTIKA
ATTIC

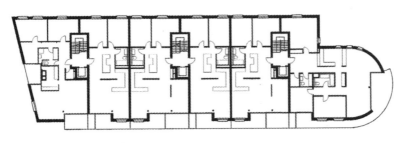

ZWEITES OBERGESCHOSS
THIRD FLOOR PLAN

0   25

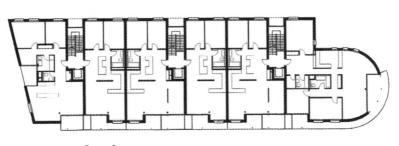

ERSTES OBERGESCHOSS
SECOND FLOOR PLAN

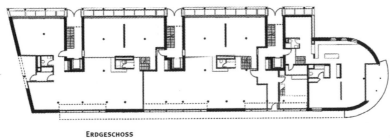

ERDGESCHOSS
FIRST FLOOR PLAN

Fernmeldedirektion Bern
Telecommunication Direction Bern

Erdgeschoss
First floor plan

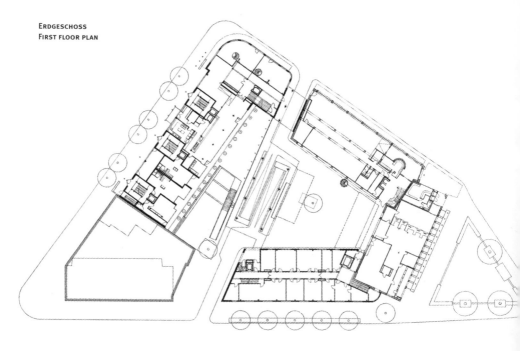

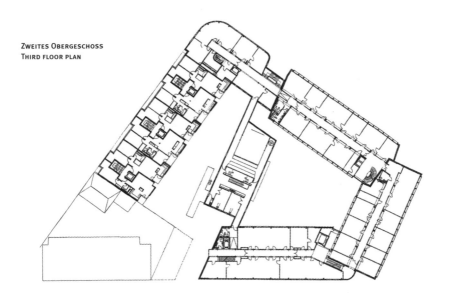

ZWEITES OBERGESCHOSS
THIRD FLOOR PLAN

N

0   25

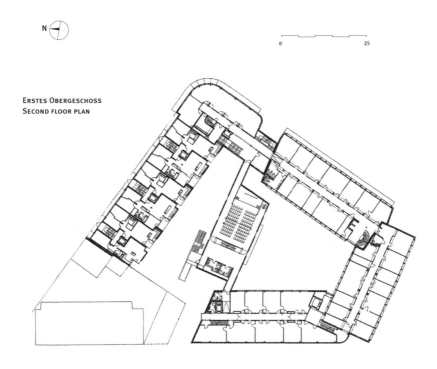

ERSTES OBERGESCHOSS
SECOND FLOOR PLAN

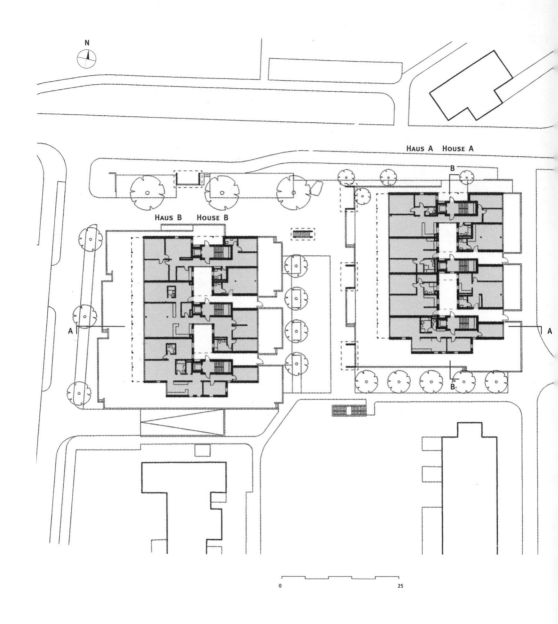

N

HAUS A HOUSE A

HAUS B HOUSE B

B

A

A

B

0   25

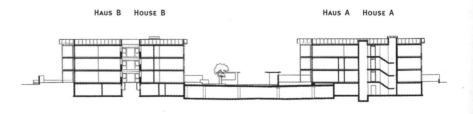

HAUS B HOUSE B

HAUS A HOUSE A

SCHNITT A – A   SECTION A – A

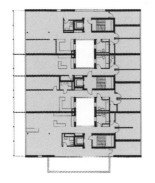

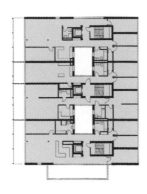

ZWEITES OBERGESCHOSS
THIRD FLOOR PLAN

HAUS B   HOUSE B

HAUS A   HOUSE A

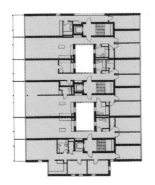

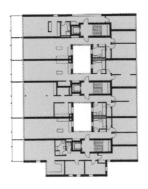

ERSTES OBERGESCHOSS
SECOND FLOOR PLAN

ATRIUMHÄUSER KALCHACKER
ATRIUM HOUSES KALCHACKER

HAUS A   HOUSE A

SCHNITT B – B   SECTION B – B

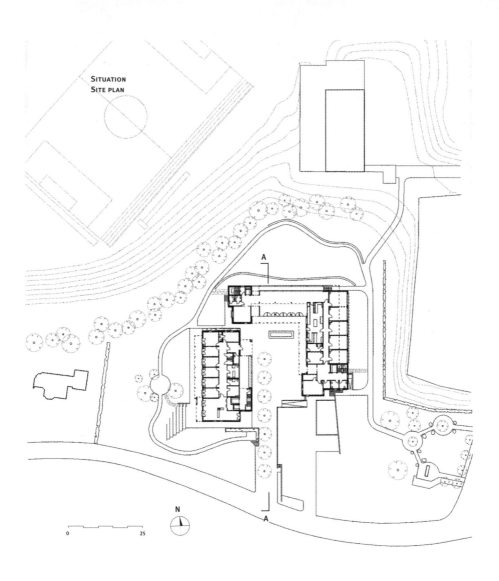

A

N

0   25

Behindertenheim La Pimpinière
Home for the Handicapped La Pimpinière

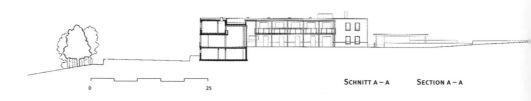

0   25

Schnitt A – A   Section A – A

134

ZWEITES OBERGESCHOSS
THIRD FLOOR PLAN

ERSTES OBERGESCHOSS
SECOND FLOOR PLAN

0   25

ERDGESCHOSS
FIRST FLOOR PLAN

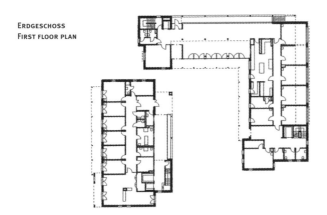

135

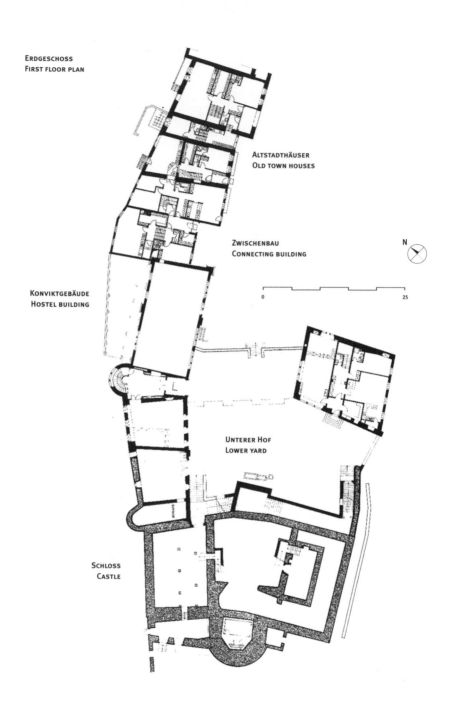

ERDGESCHOSS
FIRST FLOOR PLAN

ALTSTADTHÄUSER
OLD TOWN HOUSES

ZWISCHENBAU
CONNECTING BUILDING

KONVIKTGEBÄUDE
HOSTEL BUILDING

N

0   25

UNTERER HOF
LOWER YARD

SCHLOSS
CASTLE

SCHULHEIM SCHLOSS ERLACH
SCHOOL HOSTEL ERLACH CASTLE

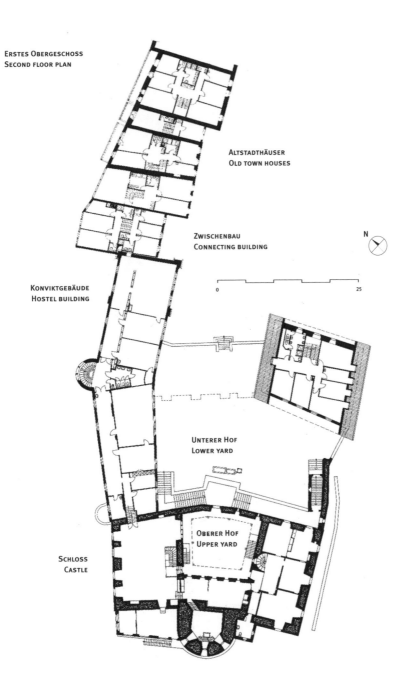

ERSTES OBERGESCHOSS
SECOND FLOOR PLAN

ALTSTADTHÄUSER
OLD TOWN HOUSES

ZWISCHENBAU
CONNECTING BUILDING

N

KONVIKTGEBÄUDE
HOSTEL BUILDING

0   25

UNTERER HOF
LOWER YARD

OBERER HOF
UPPER YARD

SCHLOSS
CASTLE

VERMONTPARK/ OBERES MURIFELD

Text Benedikt Loderer
Photos Thomas Keller (Vermontpark),
Marco Schibig (Oberes Murifeld)

Erinnerung an Vermont (1983–90), wo ich kalt geblieben. Ein Konzept, das von Duplexwohnungen ausging, wurde mit Geschosswohnungen realisiert. Trickreich, etwas überinstrumentiert. arb hat das Investorendiktat überlistet. Die privaten Aussenräume sehr sorgfältig, aber auch sehr aufwendig. Wieder taucht der Wohnwert auf, die Brauch- und Benutzbarkeit der Wohnung. Wohnwert ist eine der Kardinaltugenden von arb.

Der Wald steht grün und schweiget und bildet das Hinten der einen Zeile. Die konsequente Ausrichtung nach Süden macht das Vorne. Hier riechts nach Anwälten, Nachbarschaftsprozessen. Die Häuser sind zu teuer für den Frieden. Einspruch Aellen: «Keine Spur von Streit unter den Mietern. Die Zufriedenheit ist gross. Einzelne Mieter haben uns wissen lassen, dass ihre Wohnungen jederzeit für Besichtigungen offen stehen.»

Der Gegensatz dazu: die Sanierung der Genossenschaftswohnungen im Oberen Murifeld (1996–97). «Erneuerung à la carte» stand im Hochparterre. Peter Keller hat gezeigt, was ein geduldiger Architekt vermag. Wieviel Mitsprache braucht der Mensch oder das Zuhören als architektische Tugend, hiess das Stück. Hauptrolle: Peter Keller als Übervater. Jeder durfte mitreden, doch die Architekten mussten das Schiff steuern. Hier wird nicht Grossarchitektur gemacht, sondern Sozialreparatur. Verträglichkeitsgrenzen müssen ausprobiert werden. Welche sind die des Hauses und

Memories of Vermont (1983–90) where I was always cold. A concept presuming duplex apartments was realized with apartments. Tricky and a bit overorchestrated. arb outsmarted the investor's dictate. The private outdoor spaces, very careful but also very extravagant. Again, the living standard occurs, the usability and utilization of the apartment. Living standard is one of arb's cardinal virtues.

The forest is green and quiet and forms the back of one row. The consequential orientation towards the south forms the front. Here, it smells of lawyers, neighborhood trials. The houses are too expensive for the peace and quiet. Objection Kurt Aellen: "No sign of arguments between the tenants. The satisfaction is great. Some tenants have informed us that their apartments are open for visits at any time."

Contrary to it: the redevelopment of the cooperative apartments in Oberes Murifeld (1996–97). "Renewal à la Carte" stood in the mezzanine. Peter Keller showed what a patient architect is capable of doing. The piece was called "how much right to a say does a man need, or: listening as an architect's virtue." Lead role: Peter Keller as alter ego. Everybody had a say, but the architects had to steer the ship. Large-scale architecture isn't practiced here but instead social repair. Limits of endurance have to be tested. What are those of the house and those of the renters? What remains exciting is

welche jene der Mieter? Spannend aber bleibt, dass Vermont und Oberes Murifeld nur einige hundert Meter auseinanderliegen. Vom Denken her sind es Kilometer.

Wirklich? Denkt man an die Menge des Geldes, so bleibt der Abstand, denkt man an die Art des Umgangs damit, verringert er sich um einiges. Nochmals: Kardinaltugend Wohnwert. Der Begriff ist eindeutig mit arb verbunden. Es liegen auch etwa zehn Jahre und der Absturz der Wohnbauspekulation zwischen den beiden Projekten. Was in den achtziger Jahren neugebaut teuer werden durfte, musste 1996 umgebaut und billig sein. Anders herum: Es sind neue Aufgaben aufgetaucht. Werterhaltung ist das Stichwort, Bauerneuerung die zugehörige Tätigkeit. arb hat sich dieser Kärrnerarbeit angenommen.

that Vermont and Oberes Murifeld are only a few hundred meters apart. In terms of thinking, however, it's kilometers.

Really? If one thinks for a moment about the amount of money, the distance remains. If one thinks instead about how it's dealt with, the distance shrinks quite a bit. Again: cardinal virtue, living value. The term is clearly connected with arb. About ten years and the collapse of housing speculation boom separate both projects. What could be built new and expensive during the eighties had to be converted and cheap in 1996. The other way around: new tasks have emerged. Value preservation is the headword, building renewal the activity belonging to it. arb took care of this arduous task.

SITUATION   SITE PLAN   0 ⌐⌐⌐⌐⌐ 50

WOHNBAUTEN VERMONTPARK
APARTMENT BUILDINGS VERMONTPARK

Das ursprüngliche Projekt sah vier Bauten vor, die sich um die bestehende Villa gruppieren. Die beiden nördlichen Bauten wurden realisiert.

The original project proposed four buildings grouped around the existing villa. The two northern buildings were realized.

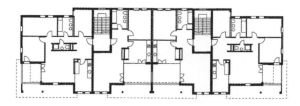

Zweites Obergeschoss
Third floor plan

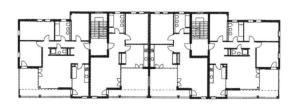

Erstes Obergeschoss
Second floor plan

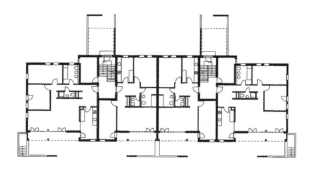

Erdgeschoss
First floor plan

Wohnbauten Vermontpark
Apartment Buildings Vermontpark

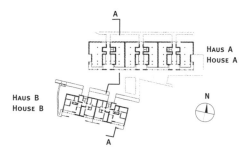

Haus A
House A

Haus B
House B

N

HAUS A   HOUSE A

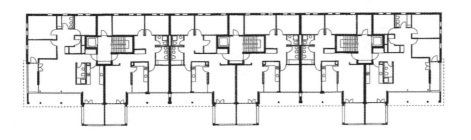

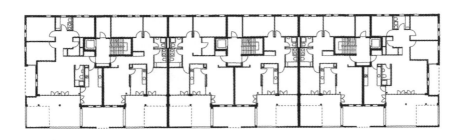

0 _____ 25

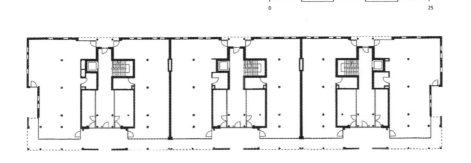

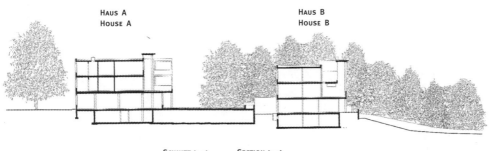

HAUS A   HAUS B
HOUSE A   HOUSE B

SCHNITT A – A   SECTION A – A

143

Seiten 144–150

VERMONTPARK

*Zwei Wohnbauten in einem
teilweise bewaldeten Park. Typisch
sind die auf den Platz gerichteten,
plastisch ausgebildeten,
den Wohnungen vorgelagerten
Zonen mit grossen, vor Einsicht
geschützten Wohn-Aussenräumen.
Hinter der Säulenreihe liegen auf
den Platz gerichtete Büroräume
und die Hauseingänge.*

Seiten 152–157

OBERES MURIFELD

*Renovation eines Quartiers mit
über siebzigjährigen Wohnhäusern.
Die MieterInnen wählten aus dem
Baukasten-Katalog die wertvermehrenden Massnahmen und
bestimmten so den Umfang der
Renovation und den zukünftigen
Mietzins selber. Dem Mieter dieser
Wohnung genügten minimale Ver-
besserungen im Bereich der Küche.
Der grösste und teuerste Eingriff
bildet die räumliche Erweiterung
seiner kleinen Zweizimmerwohnung
durch einen Balkon, von dem aus
sich der Garten überblicken lässt.*

Pages 144–150

VERMONTPARK

*Two apartment houses in a partially
wooded park. The sculptural zones
in front of the apartments oriented
towards the square with large
interior and outdoor rooms that are
protected from insights are typical
design elements. Behind the row of
columns, offices are oriented
towards the square and the
entrance doors.*

Pages 152–157

OBERES MURIFELD

*Renovation of a quarter with
apartment buildings that are over
70 years old. The tenants chose the
value-increasing measures from the
modular system catalog thus
determining both the extent of the
renovation and the future rent they
would have to pay. This tenant was
happy with minimal improvements
made to the kitchen area. The
largest and most expensive
operation was the extension of his
small two-bedroom apartment by
the addition of a balcony from
where the garden can be viewed.*

SIEDLUNG HINTERE AUMATT

Photo-Essay Peter Lüem
Text Arthur Kirchhofer, Therese Lindt Kirchhofer (A.K./T.L.)
Benedikt Loderer (B.L.)

DEVELOPMENT HINTERE AUMATT

Die Siedlung Hintere Aumatt ist nicht nur sorgfältig in die Landschaft am Wohlensee eingebettet, auch innerhalb der Siedlung und an den Rändern ist die Natur ein integrierender Bestandteil. Die Biologen Arthur Kirchhofer und Therese Lindt Kirchhofer, die das Bepflanzungskonzept entwickelt haben, beschreiben wie es dazu kam. Der Photograph Peter Lüem zeigt, wie sich die Pflanzenwelt in der Siedlung heute präsentiert.

«Warum sollte eine blumenreiche Wiese in den Bergen wunderschön, in der Stadt dagegen hässlich sein?»

Dies der Titel unseres Plädoyers für den Wildgarten in einem Tages Anzeiger Magazin von 1979. Wir, Biologiestudenten aus Bern, waren durch die Öffentlichkeitsarbeit zweier solothurnischer Lehrer auf die Idee des Naturgartens gestossen. Der reich bebilderte Artikel führte zum Kontakt mit den Architekten der arb Arbeitsgruppe. Sie waren von der Idee angetan, die Umgebung der gerade auf dem Papier entstehenden Siedlung «Hintere Aumatt» unkonventionell zu gestalten und optimal in die Umgebung einzupassen. Damals herrschten in den Hausgärten noch Rasen und Rosen, was nicht von Menschenhand gestutzt und geputzt war, galt als unordentlich. Wildpflanzen gehörten bestenfalls an den Waldrand, der Ackerdistel wurde das Absamen gar per Gesetz verboten.

Der in den siebziger Jahren begonnene Kampf gegen Cotoneasterwüsten und

The Hintere Aumatt development is not only carefully embedded into the landscape at Lake Wohlen; nature is also an integrating component inside the development and along its perimeter. The biologists Arthur Kirchhofer and Therese Lindt Kirchhofer, who developed the landscaping concept, describe how it all happened. The photographer Peter Lüem shows how the plant world in the development presents itself today.

"Why should a meadow full of flowers be beautiful in the mountains but ugly in the city?"

This was the title of our plea for the nature garden in a Tages Anzeiger magazine from 1979. As biology students from Bern, we had encountered the concept of the nature garden as a result of the public relations efforts of two teachers from Solothurn. The richly illustrated article led to a contact with the architects of the arb work group. They were intrigued with the concept of designing the surroundings of the "Hintere Aumatt" development, which was evolving on paper in an unconventional way, and of optimally integrating the development into the environment. Carefully tended lawns and rose bushes still ruled in gardens back then, and what hadn't been cleaned and cut by human hands was considered disorderly. Wild plants, at best, belonged on the edges of the forest, and to the field thistle was even forbidden by law from spreading its seeds.

Rasenmonokulturen war eine Folge des wachsenden Umweltbewusstseins und der Erkenntnis, dass die Artenvielfalt in der Natur auch dem Menschen dienlich ist: neben Ethik bietet z.B. eine dichte Hecke einheimischer Pflanzen durchaus auch Ästhetik. Die beim Jäten und Trimmen gesparte Zeit verwendet der gewiefte Naturgärtner für die Entdeckung zarter Farbkompositionen, subtiler Formenspiele und des emsigen Treibens der tierischen Nutzer und Bewohner seines Reiches.

Nur zu gerne ergriffen wir die Gelegenheit, unser theoretisches Wissen in die Praxis umzusetzen und die Umgebung der Siedlung so zu planen, dass das Grün in der Überbauung nicht nur als Gestaltungselement oder gar zum Verstecken hässlicher Bauteile dient, sondern eine Funktion als eigenständiger Kleinlebensraum erfüllt und als integrierender Bestandteil des Lebens ausserhalb der Gebäude wahrgenommen wird.

DAS BEPFLANZUNGSKONZEPT

Wichtigste Elemente im Bepflanzungskonzept waren (Hoch-)Hecken als Abschluss der Siedlung sowie als Auflockerung innerhalb der Überbauung. Über eine Zeit von acht Jahren wurden 4000 Büsche gepflanzt. Dazu kamen 200 Bäume, die einerseits in einer kleinen Parklandschaft stehen oder in die Hochhecke integriert sind, andererseits als grosse Einzelbäume Eingänge markieren oder den Innenplätzen einen eigenen Charakter verleihen. Bestehende wertvolle Le-

The battle against Cotoneaster deserts and lawn monocultures that began during the seventies was a consequence of the growing environmental awareness and the insight that the variety of species in nature also serves mankind: aside from ethics, a dense hedge consisting of regional plants, for example, also offers aesthetic value. The time saved by not having to weed and trim is used by the clever gardener for the discovery of gentle color combinations, subtle formal plays and the busy hustle and bustle of the inhabitants—insects and animals— of his realm.

We loved having the opportunity to put our theoretical knowledge into practice, to plan the environment of the development in such a way that the plantings not only function as a design element or as screens to hide ugly building parts but also serve as small, independent living spaces and are perceived as an integral component of life outside the buildings.

THE LANDSCAPING CONCEPT

The most important elements in the landscaping concept were the high hedges used to delineate the edges of the development and the livening up of the superstructure. Within eight years, 4000 bushes had been planted. Add to this the 200 trees that stand in the small park landscape, or are integrated into the high hedges, or, as large individual trees, frame entrances or provide the small squares found inside with their own character. Precious, already existing, living

bensräume (z.B. die nördlich der Siedlung am Hang liegende Magerwiese) sollten erhalten und aufgewertet werden. Spezielle Kleinbiotope (Stein- und Sandhaufen, Teich, unbepflanzte Böschungen als Ruderalstandorte) wurden gezielt als Unterschlupf für Insekten, Amphibien und Reptilien angelegt.

Gerade Linien und rechte Winkel kennt die Natur nicht. Die Umgebung der Bauten wurde daher unregelmässig gestaltet, soweit dies Baggerführer und Bauführer zuliessen.

DIE GRUNDSÄTZE

Es wurden nur einheimische Pflanzen verwendet, die in der näheren Umgebung bei ähnlichen Standortbedingungen auch natürlich vorkommen. Diese nähren und beherbergen unzählige Tiere. Grundlage bildete eine Artenliste der an Waldrändern und in Hecken vorkommenden Bäume, Sträucher und Kräuter.

Die ursprünglichen Pflanzungen und Ansaaten sollten vor allem eine natürliche Entwicklung in Gang setzen. Noch heute ändert sich das Siedlungsgrün immer wieder und passt sich neuen Bedingungen und Bedürfnissen der Bewohner an.

Auch in der späteren Pflege sollten weder Pestizide noch Kunstdünger eingesetzt werden. Die Pflanzen passen sich dem vorhandenen Nährstoffangebot an, expansive Unkräuter verschwinden meist von selber wieder.

Die Pflanzen der Siedlungsumgebung müssen ihrer Funktion entsprechend eingesetzt werden:

spaces (e.g., the meadow on the slope north of the development) were to be preserved and reevaluated. Small, special biotopes (piles of sand and stones, ponds, unplanted embankments as ruderal sites) were set up on purpose as shelters for insects, amphibians and reptiles.

Straight lines and right angles do not exist in nature. Therefore, the environment was designed in an irregular manner, at least to the extent that the excavator and contractor would allow.

THE PRINCIPLES

Only indigenous plants were used. They nourish and shelter innumerable animals. The basis for the selection of plants was a list of species of trees, shrubs and herbs that can be found at the edges of near-by forests and hedges.

The original plantings and seeds were intended to initiate natural development. Today, the flora in the development is still changing and adapting to new conditions and to the needs of the inhabitants.

In the later care of the plants, neither pesticides nor artificial fertilizer will be used. The plants should adapt to the existing nutrients in the soil, and weeds usually disappear by themselves.

The plants of the areas surrounding the development have to be used according to their function:

A dense green belt around the outer edge of the development integrates the superstructure into the surroundings and forms a "soft" transition from the hard

Ein dichter Grüngürtel um den Aussenrand der Siedlung bindet die Überbauung in die Umgebung ein und bildet einen «weichen» Übergang vom harten Material der Bauten zu Wald, Wiesen und Äckern.

Der sich mitten durch die Siedlung ziehende Grünstreifen dient der Auflockerung zwischen den Bauten und teilweise dem Sichtschutz. Zudem verbessert er – vor allem im Sommer – die mikroklimatischen Verhältnisse an der südexponierten Lage.

An einigen Stellen wurden bestimmte Pflanzen zur Stabilisierung von Böschungen in ingenieurbiologischer Bauweise verwendet.

Nicht zuletzt soll einheimisches Grün auch Auge und Herz erfreuen: austreibende Knospen im Frühling, eine Fülle von Blüten in der warmen Jahreszeit, farbige Früchte und Blätter im Herbst und bizarre Formen im Winter. Die Nistgelegenheiten und das vielfältige Nahrungsangebot locken Vögel und Insekten an. Durch die Beobachtung von Tieren direkt vor der Haustür wächst bei den Bewohnern eine Beziehung zur weiteren Umgebung, zur Umwelt. Speziell Kinder gehen in der naturnahen Umgebung auf Entdeckungsreisen, sammeln Erfahrungen und lernen den Umgang mit der «Natur» auf spielerische Weise.

Die Information der Bewohner und ihr Miteinbezogen-Werden in die Umgebungsarbeiten waren uns ein grosses Anliegen. Bei Abschluss jeder Bauetappe wurden deshalb gemeinsam mit den neu-

materials of the buildings to the forest, meadows and fields.

The green belt running through the development serves to liven up the area between the buildings and to provide a modicum of privacy. Additionally, especially during the summer, it improves the microclimatic conditions of the south-facing areas.

In some places, certain plants were used as a biological construction method in order to stabilize embankments.

Not least, the regional flora should also be pleasing to the eye and to the heart: sprouting buds in the springtime, a wealth of blossoms during the warmer months, colorful fruit and leaves in the fall and bizarre shapes during winter. The nesting possibilities and the wide variety of food attract both birds and insects. Through the observation of nature right outside their doors, the inhabitants are able to develop a relationship with their surroundings, with the environment. Children, especially, set out on journeys of discovery in this environment that is so close to nature. They gather experiences and learn to interact with "nature" in a playful way.

Educating the inhabitants and integrating them into the process of landscaping their environment were of great concern to us. Following the completion of each building phase, planting actions were therefore undertaken that included the participation of the new residents, which allowed a relationship with the green outside their homes to evolve.

en Bewohnern Pflanzaktionen durchgeführt, bei denen eine erste Beziehung zum Grün vor dem eigenen Zuhause entstehen konnte.

DIE REALITÄT

An mehreren Informationsabenden brachten wir den Bewohnern der Aumatt den Wildgarten näher. Dies ist unseres Erachtens gelungen, denn die letzte Etappe bepflanzten die Bewohner vollständig in eigener Regie. Auch die Pflege haben sie selbst in die Hand genommen und organisieren jährlich einen oder mehrere Pflegetage. Gegen ein Vorurteil konnten wir allerdings nicht ankommen: die Mütter kleiner Kinder behaupteten trotz gegenteiligem Bescheid immer wieder, die Beeren einheimischer Sträucher seien giftig. Dieses hartnäckige Gerücht wird sich wohl noch lange halten...

Unser Konzept betraf nur den allgemeinen Teil der Siedlungsumgebung. Ihre eigenen Gärtchen gestalten die Bewohner (und Besitzer) ganz nach Belieben. So entstand mit der Zeit ein reizvolles Nebeneinander von naturnaher «Wildnis» mit wuchernden Heckenrosen und intensiv betreuten Edelrosen.

Im Laufe der Jahre wurde unser Gestaltungskonzept in einzelnen Bereichen radikal verändert und von den Bewohnern den sich entwickelnden Bedürfnissen angepasst. So entstand in unserem ursprünglich geplanten parkähnlichen Wäldchen mit weit auseinanderstehenden Bäumen ein sich immer mehr ausdehnender Gemüsegarten, gesäumt

THE REALITY

During several information evenings, we acquainted the Aumatt residents with the natural garden. In our view, this was a success because they had done the planting completely on their own during the last building phase. They also took responsibility for the care of the gardens into their own hands and organized one or more workdays each year. However, we couldn't eliminate one stubborn misconception: despite information to the contrary, the mothers of small children still insist that the berries of regional shrubs are poisonous. This assertion will most likely linger for a while...

Our concept only concerned the common areas of the development's surroundings. The inhabitants (and owners) laid out their own small gardens as they pleased. With time, an attractive juxtaposition of natural "wilderness" with wildly growing hedge roses and carefully tended rose bushes developed.

Over the years, our design concept has been radically changed in some areas and adapted by the inhabitants to evolving needs. Our originally planned, small, park-like forest with trees that stood far apart from one another has become an ever-expanding vegetable garden lined by high fruit trees and a small hut village for the children. Their fathers enthusiastically participated in building the latter and they vehemently defended the collection of crooked huts made of scrap wood against the strict bureaucratic regulations.

von Hochstammobstbäumen und einem Hüttendorf für die Kinder. In letzterem bauten auch die Väter begeistert mit und verteidigten die Ansammlung schiefer Hütten aus Abfallholz vehement gegen die Auflagen einer bürokratischen Verwaltung.

Die vielfältigen Aktivitäten an einem warmen Wochenende auf den Plätzen in der Siedlung und den angrenzenden Gemüsegärten und Spielarenen zeigen, dass eine menschenfreundliche Architektur, verbunden mit einer naturnahen Umgebung auch dazu beitragen kann, die Bewohner von der allwöchentlichen Flucht ins Grüne abzuhalten. Damit wird ein weiterer Beitrag zur Erhaltung unserer Umwelt geleistet. Noch nach 20 Jahren freuen wir uns am Gesamtwerk Hintere Aumatt. Unsere Saat ist aufgegangen. (A.K./T.L.)

HINTERE AUMATT

Wir stehen auf dem kleinen Weg, und es kommen drei Damen an den Architekten vorbei. Sagt eine von den dreien: «Nenei, dasch nit dr Dorfplatz.» Für diese Bewohnerin ist also die Siedlung Hintere Aumatt (1973–92) ein Dorf. arb schreibt darüber: «Die Siedlung bildet als urbanes Gefüge einen beabsichtigten Kontrast zur ländlichen Umgebung.» Nehmen wir die Überbauung Kappelenring dazu, ein Fragment der Cité Radieuse gleich in der Nähe, so steigt die Verwirrung noch: Wo wohnt nun die Urbanität? Im Dorf, im urbanen Gefüge oder in der Ville Radieuse? (Es müsste noch die Gartenstadt, die ja längst zur «Hüsli»-Sammlung verkommen ist und in der Ge-

The various activities that take place on the squares of the development and in the adjoining vegetable gardens and playgrounds during a warm weekend shows that a people-friendly style of architecture combined with a natural environment can also help to entice the inhabitants to forgo the weekly flight into the countryside. And this is another contribution to the preservation of our environment. Twenty years later, we're still enjoying the work done in Hintere Aumatt. Our seed has germinated. (A.K./T.L.)

HINTERE AUMATT

We're standing on the small path, and three ladies pass the architects. One of them says: "No, no, that's not the village square." For this resident of the Hintere Aumatt development (1973–92) this is a village. arb writes about it: "The development, as an urban arrangement, forms an intended contrast with the rural environment." If we add the Kappelenring area, a fragment of the nearby Cité Radieuse, the confusion increases: Now, where does urbanity live? In the village, in the urban arrangement or in the Ville Radieuse? (We'd also need to consider the garden city, which has degraded into a collection of small houses and is very well at home in the community of Wohlen.)

Urbanity is less a form of living than an attitude. In Aumatt it has the necessary breath to develop—a balance between private and public space. It enables a life with a self-chosen participation. I can, but I

164

meinde Wohlen sehr wohl zu Hause ist, mitberücksichtigt werden.)

Urbanität ist wohl weniger eine Wohnform, als eine Haltung. Sie hat in der Aumatt den nötigen Atem, sich zu entfalten: Die Balance zwischen privatem und öffentlichem Raum. Sie ermöglicht ein Leben mit selbstgewählter Teilnahme. Ich kann, aber ich muss nicht. Es ist auch offensichtlich, dass sich jede Siedlung ihre Bewohner ausliest. In der Aumatt wohnen Leute wie die arb-ler. Die Aumatt hat arb ja auch für sich selbst gebaut. Genauer: aus den Trümmern des Konkurses einer Generalunternehmung hat arb das Projekt durch die Gründung einer Wohnbaugenossenschaft gerettet. arb hat sich seine Bauherrschaft selber entworfen. Es gab bereits eine rechtsgültige Planung für Rastel-Granit-Häuser der Horta AG. Diese nur wenig geänderte Planung war auch die Grundlage für das durch die Genossenschaft realisierte Projekt.

Der Hang diktiert. Das Projekt ist eine Schnittlösung. Zweimal wird eine Raumfolge in den Hang gesetzt, der Fussgängerzwischenraum unterteilt das Ensemble in einzelne «Höfe». Der Berg wird hinten steiler, was eine grosse Terrasse erlaubt. Gubbio, dachte ich, ein Erinnerungsanflug. Die Hintere Aumatt ist für mich das Projekt, das arb am deutlichsten verkörpert. Wahrscheinlich auch das, in dem am meisten Herzblut steckt. (Fast 20 Jahre floss es!) Dürfte ich den Architekturtouristen nur eines zeigen, es wäre die Hintere Aumatt, nicht der Merzenacker, selbst wenn der Merzenacker architektonisch viel ehrgeiziger ist. (B.L.)

don't have to. It's also obvious that each development selects its residents. In Aumatt live people like the arb members. After all, arb built Aumatt for themselves. To be more precise: from the ruins of the bankruptcy of a general contractor, arb rescued the project by founding a housing cooperative. arb designed their own building ownership. A legally valid plan for Rastel granite houses of Horta AG already existed. This slightly modified plan was the basis for the project realized by the cooperative.

The slope dictates. The project is a section solution. A spatial sequence is placed into the slope two times; the pedestrian space divides the ensemble into individual "farms." The mountain rises in the back, allowing for a large terrace. Gubbio, I thought, a trace of memory.

Hintere Aumatt, to me, is the project that most clearly impersonates arb. And probably the one containing the most heart blood. (It flowed for almost 20 years!) If I could show the architecture tourists only one, it would be Hintere Aumatt and not Merzenacker, even though Merzenacker is much more ambitious in an architectural sense. (B.L.)

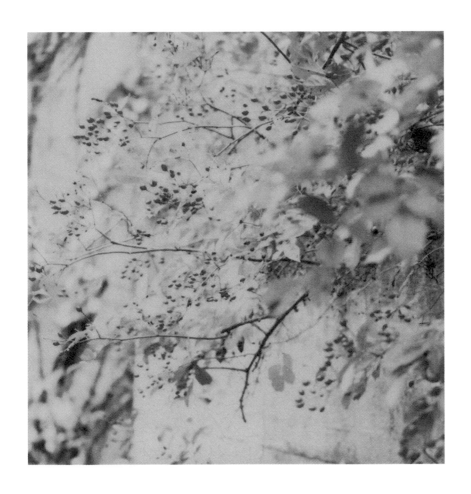

182

Hintere Aumatt

Aus der Vogelschau zeigt sich die klare Struktur: zwei langgestreckte Fussgängerzonen werden von Baukörpern flankiert. Quergestellte Bauten unterteilen diesen Aussenraum und bilden verschieden gestaltete hofartige Abschnitte. Zum Bepflanzungskonzept gehören die Magerwiese im Norden und der Grünzug der mitten durch die Siedlung läuft.

HINTERE AUMATT

An aerial view shows the clear structure: two long pedestrian zones are flanked by building volumes. Buildings placed at right angles divide this outdoor space and form yard-like segments with various designs. The meadow to the north, and the green belt running through the development are part of the landscaping concept.

187

Hintere Aumatt

Nord-Süd-Schnitt durch die untere Wohnzeile
North-South section through the bottom row of apartments

Quergestellter
Baukörper

Building volume
placed at right angle

Reihenhaus mit Garten
Row house with garden

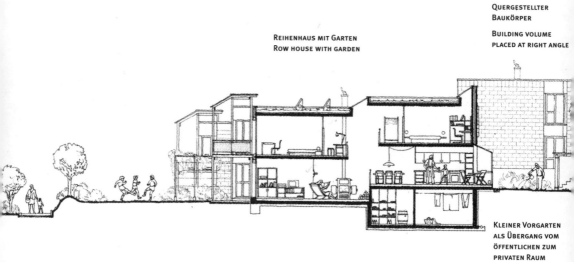

Kleiner Vorgarten
als Übergang vom
öffentlichen zum
privaten Raum

Small front garden
as a transition
from public
to private space

GRÜNZUG
GREEN BELT

MAGERWIESE
MEADOW

UNTERE WOHNZEILE
BOTTOM ROW OF APARTMENTS

GESCHOSSWOHNUNGEN
MIT GROSSEN AUSSENRÄUMEN

FULL-FLOOR APARTMENTS WITH
LARGE OUTDOOR SPACES

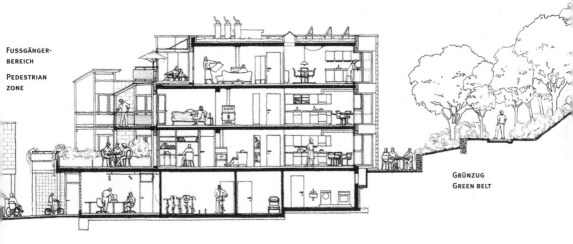

FUSSGÄNGER-
BEREICH

PEDESTRIAN
ZONE

GRÜNZUG
GREEN BELT

SÄULENGANG UND ATELIER
IM SOCKELGESCHOSS

COLONNADE AND STUDIO ON
FIRST FLOOR

0   10

Hintere Aumatt

Haus mit zwei übereinander-
liegenden Duplexwohnungen
mit Balkonen und Gärten

House with two duplex
apartments above one another,
with balconies and gardens

Quergestellter
Baukörper

Building volume placed
at a right angle

Fussgänger-
bereich

Pedestrian
zone

Blick auf einen Quer-
gestellten Baukörper

View of a building
volume placed at a
right angle

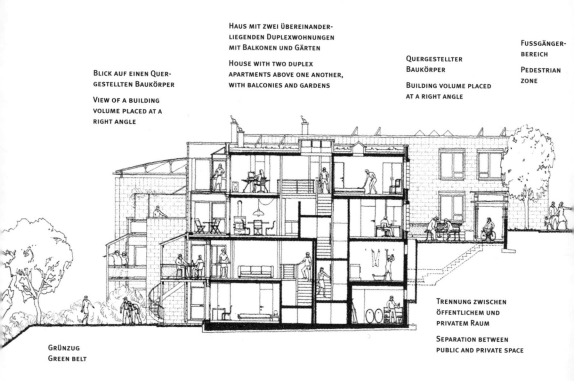

Trennung zwischen
öffentlichem und
privatem Raum

Separation between
public and private space

Grünzug
Green belt

190

GRÜNZUG
GREEN BELT

MAGERWIESE
MEADOW

OBERE WOHNZEILE
TOP ROW OF APARTMENTS

DUPLEXWOHNUNG MIT
TERRASSE UND ZWEI GESCHOSS-
WOHNUNGEN MIT BALKONEN

DUPLEX APARTMENT WITH TERRACE
AND TWO FULL-FLOOR APARTMENTS
WITH BALCONIES

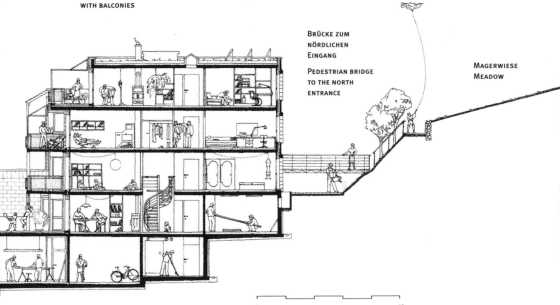

BRÜCKE ZUM
NÖRDLICHEN
EINGANG

PEDESTRIAN BRIDGE
TO THE NORTH
ENTRANCE

MAGERWIESE
MEADOW

SÄULENGANG VOR EINEM
ATELIER IM ERDGESCHOSS

COLONNADE IN FRONT OF A
STUDIO ON THE FIRST FLOOR

0   10

191

DIE HERRSCHAFT DER MECHANI-SIERUNG[1]

Text Benedikt Loderer   Photos Thomas Keller

MECHANIZATION TAKES COMMAND[1]

SCHANZENPOST

Eine Erbschaft vom Bahnhofsneubau her, die Stellung längs der Schanzenbrücke war immer schon etwas unglücklich, das Gebäude «säuft ab» gegen die Strassensteigung. Der PTT von damals war das kein Anliegen, sie wollten einen Industriebau. Was immerhin zu einer kleinteiligen, unprätentiösen Fassade geführt hat. Die Mechanik des Sortierens brauchte eine Hülle, das war alles. Die Schalter, der Publikumsbereich überhaupt, waren nicht entscheidend. Anhängsel und eigentlich der Sorgfalt kaum wert.

Heute heisst das neue Gesellschaftsspiel Kundenfreundlichkeit, und dafür mussten die Schalter erneuert und erweitert werden. Welche Atmosphäre braucht der Freund Kunde? arb nähert sich der Bank. Ziemlich kühl, metallisch, gläsern. Die Post ist modern, sowieso, sie muss aber auch die kommerzielle Dekorationswut ertragen können. Es ist also klug, zurückhaltend zu bleiben. Die Lichtführung, einmal mehr, ist besonders wichtig. In der Decke der verlochten Passage vor den Schaltern leuchtet nun ein Oberlichtstreifen. Über den Schaltern eine Lichtfuge mit Glaslamellen. Im neuen Postfachraum raffinierte Lichtfässer in der Decke. (Diese Fächergruft – sauber, reformiert und ordentlich, ein Ort, an dem man den Fremden die Schweiz zeigen kann.) Doch wiederum nicht der Publikumsbereich ist entscheidend, sondern

1. In «Die Herrschaft der Mechanisierung» (Athenäum, Frankfurt am Main 1987) untersucht Sigfried Giedion was die industrielle Produktion für Folgen hat. Speziell was geschieht, wenn sie auf organische Substanz stösst und versucht, diese zu meistern.

SCHANZENPOST

A legacy of the new station building, the situation along Schanzenbrücke has always been a bit unfortunate, the building "drowns" in the rising street level. PTT (the post office) wasn't concerned about it back then; they wanted an industrial building. And this fact, at least, led to a small-scale, unpretentious façade. The mechanism of sorting needed a shell, and that was all. The counters, the entire public area, weren't convincing; they were merely add-ons, hardly worth the bother.

Today, the new social game is called customer service, and for this purpose the counters had to be redesigned and expanded. What kind of atmosphere does our friend, the customer, need? arb approaches the bench. Rather cool, metallic, glazed. The post office is modern anyway, but it also has to be able to stand up to the commercial decoration rage. It is therefore smart to remain reserved. The lighting is, once again, especially important. Now, a skylight strip is shining down from the ceiling of the perforated passage in front of the counters, and above the counters, a light joint with glass strips. In the new room housing the post office boxes, there are very clever light barrels in the ceiling. (This mailbox mausoleum—clean, reformed and orderly, a place where one can show off Switzerland to the foreigner.) But again,

1. In "Mechanization takes command" (Oxford University Press, Inc., 1948). Siegfried Giedion examines the consequences of industrial production, especially what happens if it encounters organic substance and tries to master it.

die Triage. Die Maschinen werden klüger und schneller, der Bau hinkt hintennach. Sanieren, Umbauen und Erweitern. Probleme lösen, keine Welt erfinden. Die Post arbeitet weiter, Tag und Nacht, eine Million Briefe in 24 Stunden, ein Strom, der in Schleusen, Haltebecken, Düsen, Filter gelenkt werden muss. Baue fliessend um und an. Nie darf die Post stillstehen.

Begonnen hatte alles mit Unterhaltsarbeiten, arb wurde Oberhausabwart. Daraus entwickelten sich Studien, Konzepte, irgend einmal genügte Flicken nicht mehr, man musste Sanieren. Sanieren ist eine intellektuelle Tätigkeit, wer saniert, will nicht das Ursprüngliche wiederherstellen, er will das Vorhandene verbessern. Die Werterhaltung ist notwendig, aber nicht ausreichend. Darum ist nicht bloss saniert, sondern auch umgebaut und erweitert worden. Eine neue Post entstand aus dem Skelett der alten. Auch hier musste die angewandte Vernunft in Betrieb gesetzt werden. Trotzdem: Vernunft ist notwendig, aber nicht ausreichend, erst ein kräftigerer Schuss Erfindergeist macht aus der Analyse ein Projekt. arb saniert, baut um, erweitert.

PAKETVERARBEITUNGSZENTREN

Hier geht es um Bauherrenarbeit. Architektur machen, hiess Architektur möglich machen. arb unterstützte die Abteilung Immobilien Post (IMP) als Leiter eines «Supportteams Bau» bei der Generalplanersubmission, der Standortevaluation und den Vorbereitungen für den

the public area is not decisive but a triage. The machines become smarter and faster, but the building lags behind. Redeveloping, converting and expanding. Solving problems instead of inventing a world. The post office continues to work, day and night, one million letters in 24 hours, a stream that needs to be guided into floodgates, holding basins, nozzles and filters. Convert and add-on in a fluent way. The post office can never stand still.

It all started with maintenance work; arb became the chief caretaker. From these developed studies, concepts, at some point restorative, no longer sufficed; redevelopment was needed. Redevelopment is an intellectual act; those who redevelop have no desire to restore the original but rather to improve the existing. Value preservation is necessary but not sufficient. A new post office emerged from the skeleton of the old. Here, too, applied reasoning needed to be set into motion. Still: reason is necessary but not sufficient—only a stronger injection of innovative spirit turns pure analysis into a concrete project. arb redevelops, converts, expands.

PACKAGE HANDLING CENTERS

The task here is client work. Making architecture meant making architecture possible. arb supported the department Immobilien Post (IMP) as head of a "construction support team" in submitting the general plan, the site evaluation and the preparations for the property pur-

Landkauf. Alles eigentlich «vorarchitektonische» Aufgaben, Beratungsmandate, keine Entwurfsaufträge. Erst die Vorabklärungen für das Baubewilligungsverfahren und die Machbarkeitsstudien fallen in den Bereich dessen, was früher einmal Vorprojekt hiess. Für die Baugesuche erarbeitete arb die Eingabeprojekte. Der architektonische Gestaltungsspielraum allerdings war eng, trotzdem konnte die Qualität der Bauten wesentlich beeinflusst werden. Die Architekten operierten als eng in das Projektmanagement eingebundene Bauherrenberater und Architekturfürsprecher. Herausgestrichen wird dabei das «unübliche Tempo», sprich die kurze Zeit vom point of no return zur Baubewilligung. Die Standortbeurteilung der drei Verteilzentren begann im Frühjahr 1996, darauf mussten sechs Baueingaben, für jede Region zwei Standorte, erarbeitet werden. Die Ausführungsstandorte waren im Frühjahr 1997 bewilligt und die Bauten durch den Generalunternehmer bis Ende 1998 erstellt. Der Betrieb wurde im April 1999 aufgenommen. Produktionssteigerung heisst, schneller zu Resultaten kommen. arb «begleitet die strategische Phase», wird zur Hebamme des Projektes.

chase. All of them are really "pre-architectural" or consulting tasks, and no design commissions were involved. Only the preliminary descriptions for the building permits and feasibility studies can be categorized as part of what was once called pre-project. arb worked out the projects for the building permit applications. The architectural elbowroom was, however, rather tight, and yet the quality of the buildings could be decisively influenced. The architects operated as consultants who were closely integrated into the project management and as architectural advocates. The "unusual speed", i.e., the short time from the point of no return to the building permit, is what stands out. The site evaluation of the three distribution centers began in the spring of 1996. After that, six building petitions, for every region two locations, had to be elaborated. The locations were approved in the spring of 1997, and the buildings were consttructed by the general contractor by the end of 1998. Operations were taken up in April 1999. An increase in production means obtaing results in a quicker fashion. arb, "escorting" the strategic phase, became the midwife of the project.

Seiten 196–203

SCHANZENPOST

Erbaut in den sechziger Jahren
von der Architektengemeinschaft
Schanzenpost, in den neunziger
Jahren von arb erweitert, umgebaut
und saniert.

Seiten 204-207

SCHANZENPOST

Immer mehr Pakete und Briefe
müssen immer schneller sortiert,
eingesackt und verladen werden.
Die Herrschaft der Mechanisierung
prägt die Arbeit der Architekten. Die
räumlichen Bedürfnisse werden von
den Anlagen definiert, der Architekt
baut fliessend um.

Pages 196–203

SCHANZENPOST

Built during the sixties by the
architects' community Schanzenpost, extended, converted and
redeveloped by arb during
the nineties.

Pages 204–207

SCHANZENPOST

Ever more packages and letters
have to be assorted, bagged and
loaded ever more quickly. The
command of mechanization
influence the architects' work.
The needs are defined by the
systems, the architect converts
in a flowing way.

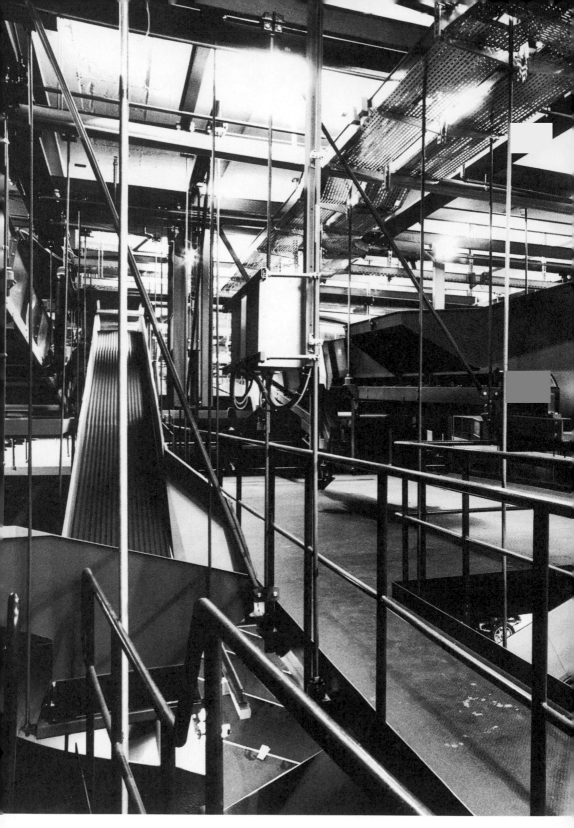

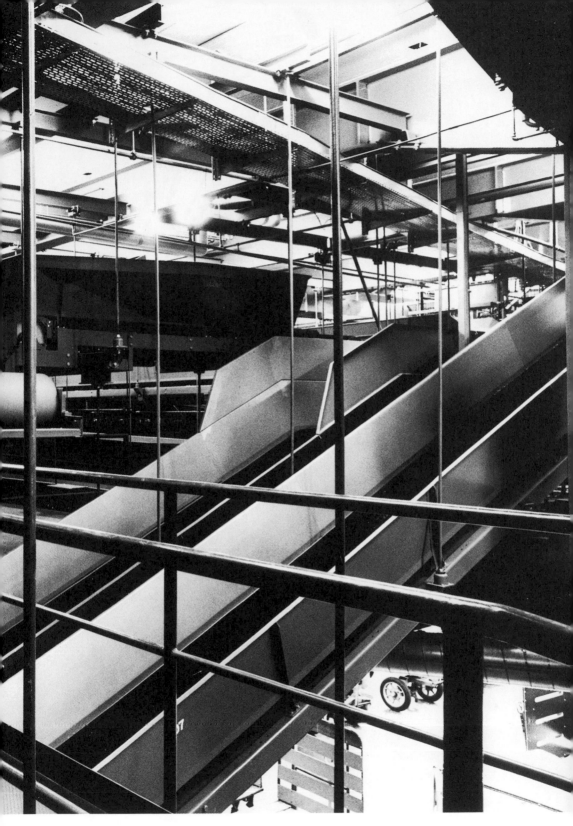

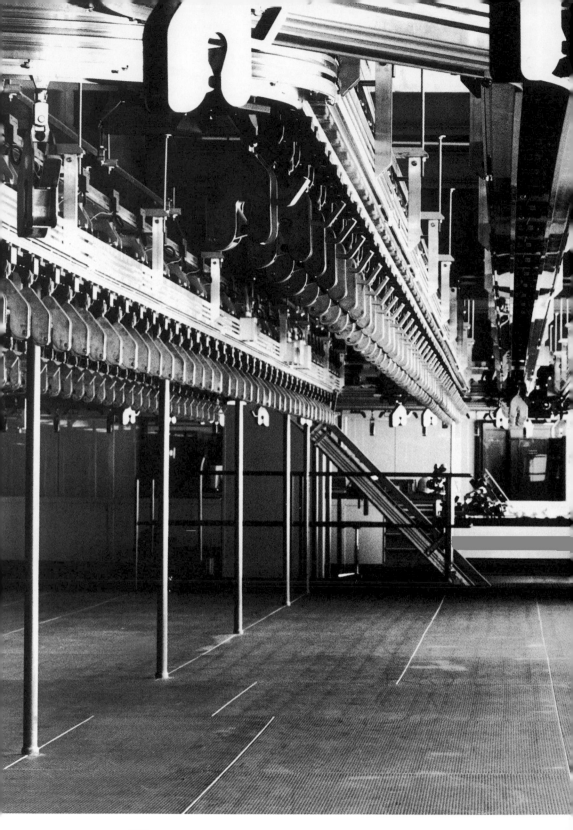

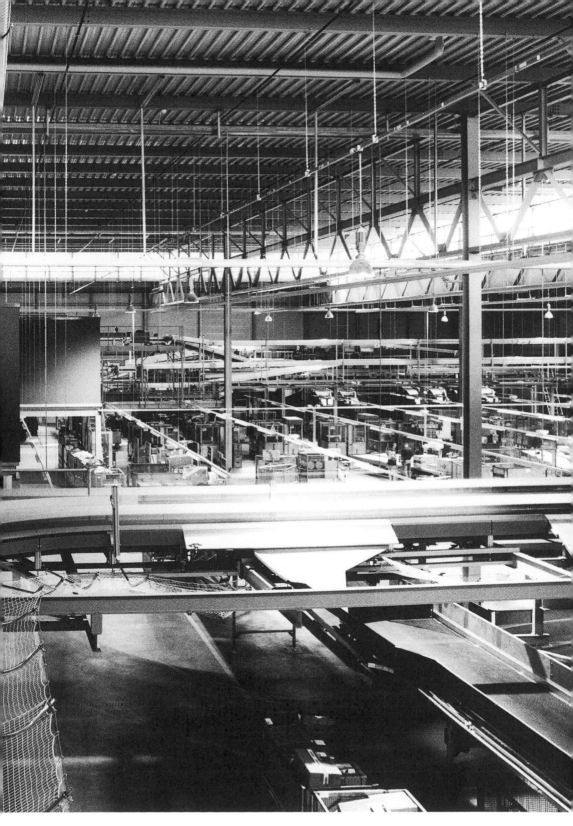

Seiten 208–213

Seiten 208–213

PAKETVERARBEITUNGSZENTREN

*Die grossen Schweizer
Paketzentren lagen in den grossen
Städten. Neu liegen sie an den
verkehrsstrategisch wichtigen
Punkten in Frauenfeld, Härkingen
und Daillens. Mechanisierung und
Logistik werden als ein Ganzes
begriffen. arb hat zusammen mit
dem Generalplaner, Emch & Berger
innerhalb eines Jahres das Konzept
formuliert, die Baubewilligungsverfahren bearbeitet und die
architektonischen Grundentscheide
gefällt. Realisiert wurden die
Zentren durch die Generalunter-
nehmen Zschokke und HSM.*

Pages 208–213

PACKAGE HANDLING CENTERS

*The large Swiss package centers
used to be in the large cities.
Now they're located at the
strategically important traffic
routes in Frauenfeld, Härkingen
and Daillens. Mechanization
and logistics are understood as
a whole. Together with the
general planner, Emch & Berger,
arb formulated the concept within
a year, worked on the building
permits and made the basic
architectural decisions.
The centers were realized by
the general contractors
Zschokke and HSM.*

CATALOG

Der Catalog stellt eine Auswahl der ausgeführten Bauten sowie Projekte und Studien von arb vor. Die Reihenfolge ist chronologisch. Sie beginnt mit den neuesten Arbeiten.

Alle in diesem Buch vorgestellten Bauten, Projekte und Studien wurden in unterschiedlichem Masse, zum Teil jedoch ganz wesentlich, auch von Einzelpersonen der arb Arbeitsgemeinschaft geprägt. Die vier Partner tragen zwar das unternehmerische Risiko – als Urheberin der Projekte zeichnet jedoch die Arbeitsgemeinschaft als Ganzes. Deshalb haben wir darauf verzichtet, Namen von einzelnen Personen der Arbeitsgemeinschaft aufzuführen. Ausnahmen sind die externen Mitarbeiter und die ehemaligen Partner von arb.

Folgende Abkürzungen werden verwendet:

A   = Adresse
P   = Projekt
P/R = Projekt und Realisation
R   = Realisation

The catalog presents a selection of the realized buildings as well as projects and studies. The sequence is in chronological order. It begins with the most recent work.

All buildings, projects and studies presented in this book were determined at differing degrees, partially in an essential way, also by individuals of arb work group. The four partners carry the entrepreneurial risk – but the work group as a whole holds the copyright to the projects. Therefore, we haven't listed names of the individuals in the work group in the catalog. Exceptions are the external collaborators and the former partners of arb.

The following abbreviations have been used:

A   = Address
P   = Project
P/R = Project and realization
R   = Realization

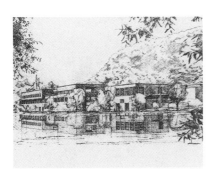

ARA Bern-Neubrück
1999 Wettbewerb/Competition

Telekommunikationsturm Hanoi
Hanoi Telecommunication Tower
1998 Wettbewerb/Competition

Im Rahmen einer Totalunternehmer-Ausschreibung bearbeiten wir die architektonische Umsetzung einer neu zu erstellenden, biologischen Reinigungsanlage. Das Betriebsgelände liegt am Aarebogen hinter dem kleinen Bremgartenwald. Das Projekt thematisiert die Auseinandersetzung zwischen klar ablesbaren Gebäuden und der sie umgebenden Landschaft, die Verknüpfung des Gebauten mit der Vegetation, die dieses umgibt und teilweise in Besitz nimmt. Die entlang der Aare verlaufenden Gebäudefluchten bilden eine klare Abgrenzung zwischen dem Spazierweg an der Aare und dem Betriebsgelände.

Within the framework of an invitation to total contractors, we worked on the architectural realization of a new biological cleaning system. The facility grounds are situated at the bend of the Aare River behind the small Bremgarten forest. The project dealt with the confrontation between clearly legible buildings and their surroundings, the connection of the architecture with the flora that surrounds and partially claims it. The building alignments along the Aare River form a clear deemarkation between the pedestrian pathway along the river and the facility grounds.

P: arb, in Totalunternehmung Losag AG, Alpha AG/OTV, Bonnard & Gadel AG
A: Neubrückstrasse, Bern

In einer weiten Ebene am Rande Hanois ist ein 400m hoher Sende- und Empfangsturm geplant, dessen Umgebung durch Freizeit- und Kulturanlagen ergänzt wird. Wir stellen den Turm in ein künstliches Bassin, in dem sich die kahle, filigrane Tragstruktur für die technischen Anlagen spiegelt. Etwa auf halber Höhe befindet sich ein Dach-Restaurant mit Aussichtsplattform. Der Besucher nähert sich dem Turm über eine weite, leicht ansteigende Ebene und erreicht dessen Fuss über einen Steg.

On a wide plain at the edge of Hanoi, a 400-meter-high broadcasting and reception tower is planned. Its environment is complemented by leisure and cultural complexes. We place the tower into an artificial basin that reflects the bare filigree supporting structure for the technical installations. Approximately halfway up the structure there is a restaurant with an observation deck. The visitor approaches the tower from a wide, gently ascending plane and reaches its base via a pedestrian bridge.

P: Palisades Vietnam arb/Lê Cuong mit/with Structures Ile-de-France, Paris – Ho Chi Minh City, A: Hanoi, Vietnam

Verwaltungsgebäude City West
Administrative Building City West
1994 Wettbewerb/Competition
1998–99 Bau/Construction

Atriumhäuser Kalchacker
Atrium Houses Kalchacker
1995–97 Projekt/Project
1998–99 Bau/Construction

Nebst der Sanierung in energetisch-ökologischer sowie in bau- und haustechnischer Hinsicht, werden eine architektonische Aufwertung und eine Nutzungsoptimierung gefordert. Zudem drängt sich eine städtebauliche Aufwertung des Gesamtkomplexes City West auf. Mit dem Projekt «Less & More» haben wir uns dazu bekannt, bei der Sanierung nur das zu tun, was für den weiteren Lebenszyklus des Baus wirklich nötig ist: less. Es bleibt aber die Freiheit, dort mehr zu tun, wo es gesamtheitlich betrachtet sinnvoll ist: more.

Aside from an energetic and ecological redevelopment, as well as with respect to the building and house technology, an architectural upgrading and optimization of the utilization were requested. Additionally, an urban upgrading of the entire complex, City West, suggested itself. With the "Less & More" project, we acquiesced to only doing what was really essential for the continuing life cycle of the building – which is less. Yet the liberty remains to do more where it makes sense in the overall situation.

P/R: arb mit interdisziplinärem Planerteam/with interdisciplinary team of planners, A: City West, Bern

Zwei Atriumhäuser bilden den nördlichen Abschluss einer bestehenden zweigeschossigen Wohnsiedlung. Lage und Volumen der beiden Häuser sind planerisch bereits vorgegeben. Wir leiten daraus dreigeschossige kompakte Baukörper ab, mit je zwei offenen Innenhöfen. Die Gebäude mit ihren 24 Meter tiefen Grundrissen werden aus verschiedenen Himmelsrichtungen natürlich belichtet. Die ungewöhnliche Dimension erzeugt Spannung und verleiht den Wohnungen Grosszügigkeit.

Two atrium houses form the northern termination of an existing, two-story housing development. The location and volume of both houses were stipulated by the given plan. From it we derived three-story, compact building volumes with two inner courtyards each. The buildings, with their 24-m-deep ground plans, are naturally lit from different directions. The unusual dimension creates suspense and provides the apartments with a large-scale character.

P/R: arb, A: Kalchackerstrasse 23/25, Bremgarten bei Bern

218

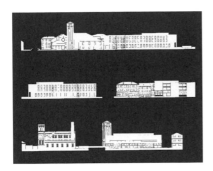

Architekturschule Venedig
Architecture School Venice
1998 Wettbewerb/Competition

Im Hafenbereich San Basilio, am Giudecca-Kanal, sollen Neubauten für das «Istituto Universitario di Architettura» entworfen werden. Ein grosses Auditorium, Konferenz- und Ausstellungsräume, Restaurant und Bar etc. werden auch der Öffentlichkeit zugänglich sein. Unser Projekt versucht in einem angepassten Massstab das in Venedig allgegenwärtige Beziehungsnetz von Plätzen und Gebäuden, Brücken und Kanälen, offenen Räumen und Parkanlagen weiterzuspinnen.

New buildings for the Istituto Universitario di Architettura are to be designed in the harbor area San Basilio at the Giudecca canal. A large auditorium, conference and exhibition spaces, restaurant, bar, etc, should also be accessible to the public. Our project tries to continue weaving the ever-present network of Venice's squares and buildings, bridges and canals, open spaces and parks in an appropriate scale.

P: arb mit/with Pius Flury, Erlenbach, Büro Z, Zürich, Weber + Saurer, Solothurn, Viewline, Solothurn
A: San Basilio, Venedig

Verwaltungssitz Valiant Holding
Administrative Headquarters
Valiant Holding
1998 Umbau/Conversion

Für das 1920 erstellte Verwaltungsgebäude drängt sich eine radikale Erneuerung auf. Der Bau soll seine ursprünglich einfache Grundstruktur wieder erhalten. Die Auftraggeberin will kein «protziges» Bankgebäude. Vielmehr soll vornehme Zurückhaltung und Bescheidenheit das Erscheinungsbild der Regionalbank prägen. In diesem Sinne werden bloss die Eingangshalle, das Treppenhaus und das grosse Sitzungszimmer repräsentativ ausgestaltet. Der Auftrag erfolgte Mitte April – Ende September ist das Gebäude bezugsbereit.

A radical renewal suggests itself for the administrative building erected in 1920. The building was to regain its simple basic structure. The client didn't want an "ostentatious" bank building. Moreover, elegant discretion and modesty was to characterize the appearance of the regional bank. In this sense, only the entrance hall, the staircase and the large conference room were designed in a representative way. The order was placed in mid-April – by end September the building could be occupied.

P/R: arb, A: Laupenstrasse 7, Bern

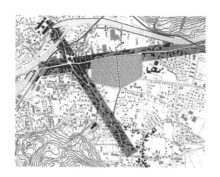

Gestaltungs- und
Verkehrskonzept Bödeli
Design and Traffic Concept Bödeli
1998 Wettbewerb/Competition

Für die Gestaltung der öffentlichen Verkehrsräume im Bödeli, Interlaken wird eine städtebauliche Leitidee gesucht. Das Bödeli soll dabei ein eigenständiges Gesicht erhalten, ohne dass der Charakter der drei Orte Matten, Interlaken und Unterseen verloren geht. Die Kernidee unseres Vorschlags heisst Reduktion: Hervorheben von zwei Achsen, Gestaltung eines Höhenwegs und von Land-Marks an den Ortseingängen. Als touristische Attraktion wird ein «Interlaken World Panorama» vorgeschlagen.

For the design of the public traffic routes in the Bödeli, Interlaken, an urban guiding idea is wanted. The Bödeli should get its individual expression without loosing the character of the three towns Matten, Interlaken and Unterseen. The core concept of our proposal is called reduction: emphasizing of two axes, design of a pathway above, along the mountains and landmarks at the town entrances. An "Interlaken World Panorama" is suggested as a tourist attraction.

P: arb mit/with Büro Z, Zürich, Christian Süsstrunk, Erlenbach, Martin Dickmann, Hannover, Atelier Roger Pfund, Carouge, A: Interlaken

Mittlerer Limmatquai Zürich
1997 Wettbewerb/Competition

Der Limmatquai als innerstädtischer Flussraum soll durch eine Umnutzung und Neugestaltung aufgewertet werden. «Das Besondere sichtbar machen» ist unsere Devise. Durch präzise und subtile Interventionen wird die Beziehung zwischen Stadt und Fluss wiederhergestellt, damit das Leben an den Flusssaum zurückkehren kann. Die Ufer-Stirnseite wird verglast. Tagsüber spiegeln sich darin Himmel und Wasser, nachts wird sie zum leuchtenden Band.

Limmatquai as an inner-city river space is to be upgraded through a reutilization and redesign. "Making visible that which is special" is our motto. Through precise and subtle interventions, the relationship between city and river is reestablished so that life can return to the riverbank. The front facing the riverbank is glazed-in. During daylight hours, the sky and water are reflected, and at night it becomes a shining band.

P: arb mit/with Büro Z, Zürich, Pius Flury, Erlenbach, Viewline, Solothurn, Weber + Saurer, Solothurn, A: Limmatquai, Zürich

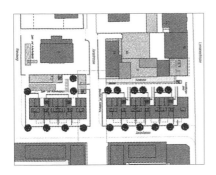

Vordere Lorraine
1997 Studie/Study

In einem wettbewerbsartigen Verfahren sucht die Stadt Bern nach geeigneten Partnern für die baurechtliche Übernahme von Liegenschaften auf einem Areal in der Lorraine. Unsere Devise heisst «Ausgleich». Neu zu erstellende Wohnbauten helfen die Grundrente der Altbauten zu entlasten. Damit kann dort weiterhin mit bescheidenem Komfort und bezahlbaren Mieten gewohnt und gearbeitet werden. Vorgeschlagen wird nicht eine definitive bauliche Lösung, sondern das Auslösen eines Prozesses.

The city of Bern, in a procedure similar to a competition, was looking for suitable partners, to lease from the city. Our motto was "compensation." Newly built apartment houses would help to relieve the property taxes of the old buildings. This would lead to the possibility to continue to live and work there with a modest level of comfort and affordable rents. What we proposed is not a definite architectural solution but rather the initiation of a process.

P: arb, A: Jurastrasse 1–5, Lorrainestrasse 15–17, Bern

Behindertenheim La Pimpinière
Home for the Handicapped
La Pimpinière
1994–95 Wettbewerb/Competition
1997–98 Bau/Construction

Das an einem Nordhang gelegene Heim bietet Schwerbehinderten ein Zuhause. Durch zwei eigenständige Gebäude wird der private vom öffentlichen Raum getrennt. Wohnhaus und Gemeinschaftsgebäude werden über einen zentralen Hof erschlossen. Während der öffentliche Charakter der Cafeteria durch eine grossflächig verglaste Fassade unterstrichen wird, sind Werkstätten und Therapiezimmer bewusst weg vom Hof, zur Landschaft hin orientiert.

The institution located on a northern slope offers a home to severely handicapped people. Two independent buildings separate the private spaces from the public spaces. The apartment house and the communal buildings are accessible via a central courtyard. While the public character of the cafeteria is enhanced by a large-scale glazed façade, the workshops and therapy rooms are consciously oriented away from the courtyard and towards the landscape.

P/R: arb, A: Malleray-Bévilard

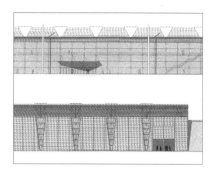

Städtische Reitschule
Municipal Riding-School
1982–83, 1987 Studien/Studies
1997–98 Projekt/Project

Unsere Studie zu den Nutzungsmöglich-
keiten und Sanierungserfordernissen der
Städtischen Reitschule zeigt, dass ebenso
wichtig wie das Nutzungskonzept selbst
das Aufzeigen des Weges ist, wie dieses
realisiert werden kann. Wir schlagen vor,
die Grosse Halle als «gedeckte Allmend»
zu nutzen und diese sowie alle anderen
Räumlichkeiten sukzessive so auszubauen,
dass ein grosser Nutzungsspielraum offen
bleibt. Fünfzehn Jahre nach den ersten Studien erfolgt der Projektauftrag für die Ge-
samterneuerung der Anlage.

Our study on the possibilities for the utilization and the requirements of the redevelopment of the municipal riding-school re-
veals that showing how it can be realized
is as important as the actual concept for
the utilization. We suggested using the riding hall as a "covered common ground"
and to extend it and all other spaces suc-
cessively in a way that allows a good deal
of elbowroom for utilization to remain
open. Fifteen years after the initial studies,
the project for the complete renewal of the
complex was commissioned.

P: arb mit/with Sylvia und Kurt Schenk,
Bern, A: Schützenmatte, Bern

Centre Radio-Télévision Sion 2006
1997 Wettbewerb/Competition

Sion kandidiert für die Olympischen Win-
terspiele 2006. Geplant ist ein neues
Radio-Televisions-Zentrum mit 30'000m²
Nutzfläche, das nach den Spielen unter an-
derem als gedeckter 300-Meter-Schiess-
stand genutzt werden soll. Wir schlagen eine stützenfreie Halle vor, welche Raum bietet für modulare, flexible Innenausbauten.
Diese sind anpassbar und einfach demon-
tier- und wiederverwendbar. Lage und
Orientierung der Halle respektieren die
Landschaft des Rhonetales und das umlie-
gende Biotop.

Sion is a candidate for the Olympic Winter
Games 2006. A new radio-television center
with 30,000 m² of floor space is planned.
After the Games, it will be used as a covered 300-meter shooting range, among
other things. We've proposed a hall without supports, offering space for modular,
flexible interior installations. They are
adaptable and can be simply disassembled
and reused. The location and orientation of
the hall respect the landscape of the Rhone
valley and the surrounding biotope.

P: arb mit/with CSD Sion, SRP Brig, Viewline, Solothurn, Weber + Saurer, Solothurn
A: Kaserne, Sion

DB-Güterbahnhof Basel
Freight Depot Basel
1997 Wettbewerb/Competition

Wohnbauten Dellergelände München
Apartment Buildings
Deller Grounds Munich
1996 Wettbewerb/Competition

Das 18 ha grosse Güterbahnareal der Deutschen Bahn in Basel wird für eine neue Nutzung frei. Das Wettbewerbsprogramm fordert Wohn-, Arbeits- und Infrastrukturbauten für eine ausgeglichene Nutzung. Unser Projekt schlägt eine Neudefinition des Stadtraumes vor. Das bestehende Stadtgefüge wird bis an den Rand eines grossen Parks erweitert. Dieser «Gleispark» erinnert wegen seiner Geometrie und den Spuren des Bahnareals an die vorherige Nutzung und wird zum identitätsstiftenden Ort des neuen Quartiers.

The 18-hectare freight depot grounds of Deutsche Bahn in Basel were opening up for new utilization. The competition program requested apartment, work and infrastructure buildings in order to create a balanced utilization. Our project suggested a redefinition of the urban space. The existing urban structure was extended to the edge of a large park. This "track park" reminds one of the former utilization due to its geometry and the traces of the railroad grounds and becomes an identity-providing place in the new quarter.

P: arb mit/with Büro Z, Zürich, Christian Süsstrunk, Erlenbach, Stefan Rotzler, Gockhausen, A: DB-Güterbahnhof, Basel

Es geht um Städtebau und Landschaftsplanung am Rande des Olympiageländes. Hier wird durch eine Betriebsauslagerung ein 2,3 ha grosses Gelände frei, und es bietet sich Gelegenheit, eine Wohnbebauung mit erweiterter Parklandschaft anzuordnen. Die in unserem Projekt neu geschaffene Parkanlage wird durch zwei markante Baukörper in Blickrichtung der bestehenden Bebauung räumlich gegliedert. Die Grossräumigkeit des Olympiaparks sowie das volumetrische Mass des Nachbarquartiers werden übernommen.

The task was urbanism and landscape planning at the edge of the Olympic grounds. Here, due to the departure of an enterprise, 2.3 hectares of property became available, and the opportunity arose to authorize a housing development with an extended park landscape. The newly created park in our project is spatially structured towards the visual line of the existing development through two striking building volumes. The spaciousness of the Olympic Park and the volumetric scale of the adjoining quarter were adopted.

P: arb mit/with Stefan Rotzler, Gockhausen, A: Nordmolkerei Deller, München

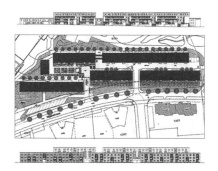

Wohnbauten Stiglenstrasse
Apartment Buildings Stiglenstrasse
1996 Wettbewerb/Competition

Die Stadt Zürich sucht mit der Kombination
von Wettbewerb und Submission Entwürfe
für kostengünstige Wohnbauten an der Stiglenstrasse. Zusammen mit dem interdis-
ziplinären Planerteam schlagen wir vor,
nicht beim Flächenangebot, sondern beim
Ausbau zu sparen. Mit auf das Einfachste
reduzierten Baukörpern wird das bestehende Quartier gegenüber den weiträumi-
gen Freiflächen abgegrenzt und gleichzeitig eine Siedlungseinheit mit allen zuge-
hörigen Nutzungen geschaffen.

By combining the competition and submission, the city of Zurich was looking for cost-
effective designs for apartment buildings
at Stiglenstrasse. Together with the interdisciplinary team of planners, we suggested ways of saving money, not with respect
to the spatial offer but to the interior design. With building volumes reduced to a
minimum, the existing quarter was demarcated from the spacious free areas and, at
the same time, a development unit with all
pertinent uses was created.

P: arb mit interdisziplinärem Planerteam/
with interdisciplinary team of planners
A: Stiglenstrasse, Zürich

Paketverarbeitungszentren
Package Handling Centers
1996 Projekt/Project
1997 Baubewilligung/Building Permit

Die Post braucht drei neue Paketzentren.
Es geht um die Beschaffung von geeigneten Grundstücken, die Errichtung von Gebäuden mit modernster Förder- und Sor-
tiertechnik sowie den Bau von Umschlag-
terminals für den kombinierten Verkehr. Wir
unterstützen die Post bei der Generalplanersubmission und bei der Evaluation der
Standorte. Wir leiten die Projektierung ein
und bearbeiten für den Generalplaner die
Baueingaben. Ein Jahr nach Arbeitsbeginn
liegen die Baubewilligungen für alle drei
Paketzentren vor.

The post office needed three new package
centers. The task was to obtain the appropriate properties, to establish buildings
with cutting-edge transport and sorting
technologies and to build handling terminals for the combined traffic. We supported the post office in the general plan submission and in the evaluation of the sites.
We initiated the projection and worked on
the building submissions for the general
planner. One year after beginning, the
building permits for all three package centers were on the table.

P/R: arb, Generalplaner: Emch + Berger,
Bern, A: Daillens, Härkingen, Frauenfeld

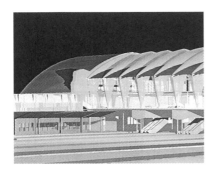

Bahnhofpasserelle Basel
Pedestrian Bridge Station Basel
1996 Wettbewerb/Competition

Schweizer Armeemuseum
Swiss Army Museum
1996 Studie/Study

Eine Passerelle zwischen der Schalterhalle und dem Südausgang im Gundeldingerquartier ist Bestandteil der Gesamtplanung des Bahnhofareals. Die Auflösung des Widerspruchs zwischen Kopfbahnhof und Durchgangsbahnhof ist Leitmotiv unseres Entwurfs. Die Passerelle wird zum Bahnhof über den Gleisen. Wir übernehmen und verlängern die Volumetrie des Schalterhallen-Daches. Dadurch erhält der Bahnhof über den Gleisen eine starke Präsenz.

A pedestrian bridge between the counter hall and the south exit in Gundeldinger quarter was an element of the overall plan for the station area. The resolution of the contradiction between the terminal station and the through-traffic station was the leitmotif for our design. The pedestrian bridge becomes a station above the tracks. We adopted and extended the volumetrics of the counter hall roof. This provides the station above the tracks with a strong presence.

P: arb mit/with Büro Z, Zürich, A: Bahnhof SBB, Basel

Das Museum zeigt die Geschichte der Schweizer Armee von 1815 bis in die Gegenwart in einer unter Denkmalschutz stehenden Pferderegieanstalt aus dem 19. Jahrhundert. Die BesucherInnen werden in den neuen Pavillon im Hof der Anlage geführt, mit Rundsicht auf das ganze Museum. Vom Pavillon führen zwei Galerien zu den Ausstellungsbereichen in den ehemaligen Stallungen und in der Reithalle. Das kommunikative Zentrum des Museums, ein Mehrzwecksaal, liegt unter der Eingangshalle.

The museum shows the history of the Swiss Army from 1815 to the present in a 19th century equestrian institute that is listed as a historic monument. The visitors are led into the new pavilion in the yard of the complex and are given a panoramic view of the entire museum. Two galleries lead from the pavilion to the exhibition spaces in the former stables and riding hall. The communicative center of the museum, a multi-purpose hall, is located below the entrance hall.

P: arb mit Atelier Roger Pfund, Carouge
A: Steffisburg

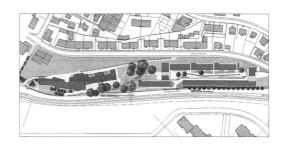

Crédit Suisse Lion d'Or
1996 Wettbewerb/Competition

Wohnbauten Schönegg
Apartment Buildings Schönegg
1996 Wettbewerb/Competition

Die Crédit Suisse will drei zusammenhängende Liegenschaften in Lausanne besser nutzen. Ein gestalterisches Gesamtkonzept soll den Eindruck eines innovativen, modernen Bankinstituts vermitteln. Der Fussgängerbereich der rue de Bourg ist mit der rue Lion d'Or zu verbinden. Unsere Intervention integriert drei Raumgruppen zu einem Ganzen, einer zusammenhängenden Passage. Einheitliche Materialien betonen die Verwandtschaft unter den einzelnen Raumgruppen. Die vorgeschlagene Passage versteht sich als eine Variation der Galerie Saint François.

The Crédit Suisse wanted to use three connected properties in Lausanne in a better way. An overall design concept was to communicate the impression of an innovative, modern banking institution. The pedestrian zone of Rue de Bourg was to be connected with the Rue Lion d'Or. Our intervention integrates three spatial groups into a whole, a connected passageway. Uniform materials enhance the relationship between the individual spatial groups. The proposed passageway is understood as a variation on the Galerie Saint François.

P: arb, A: Avenue Benjamin Constant, Lausanne

Anschliessend an das Alters- und Pflegeheim Schönegg soll eine «preisgünstige, kommunikationsfreundliche» Siedlung entstehen. Mit Gewerberäumen und Ateliers werden verschiedene Tätigkeiten und eine Öffnung nach aussen angeregt. Die Bauten unseres Projektes umgreifen im Westen den vergrösserten Park und umfassen im Osten den langgestreckten Aussenraum, der so zum Innenraum der Wohnanlage wird. Dem Fussgänger öffnen sich dadurch vom Verkehrslärm abgeschirmte alternative Wege.

A "cost-efficient, communication-friendly" development was to be created adjoining the senior citizens' residence and nursing home Schönegg. With business spaces and studios, various activities and an opening-up towards the outside were encouraged. The new buildings of our project embrace the enlarged park in the west. In the east, long, horizontal buildings surround the outdoor space, which thus becomes the interior space of the housing complex. To the pedestrian this opens alternative walkways protected from the traffic noise.

P: arb, A: Seftigenstrasse, Bern

Wohnbauten München Parsing
Apartment Buildings Munich Parsing
1995 Wettbewerb/Competition

Es geht um Städtebau und Landschaftsplanung. Eine Papierfabrik wird ausgela-
gert. Dadurch wird ein grosses Areal frei für
Wohnbauten und nicht störendes Gewerbe,
sowie für die Ausweitung des Stadtparks.
Unser Projekt gruppiert die neuen Gebäude mit Bezug zum Ort frei in die Landschaft.
Der Park als Bestandteil der Stadt und des
Grünzuges lebt vom Kontrast zwischen offenen und geschlossenen Räumen. Das
Wegnetz mit den präzise formulierten Park-
eingängen verknüpft den Park mit dem
Quartier.

The task was urbanism and landscape planning. A paper factory was moved, releasing
a large area for apartment buildings and
non-disturbing businesses as well as the
expansion of the urban park. Our project
grouped the new buildings freely into the
landscape with reference to the site. The
park as an element of the city and the green
belt lives from the contrast between the
open and enclosed spaces. The network of
pathways with the precisely formulated
park entrances connects the park with the
quarter.

P: arb mit/with Dr. Günter Schickor, Bern,
Stefan Rotzler, Gockhausen, A: Parsing,
München

Place des Nations Genève
1995 Wettbewerb/Competition

In diesem Ideenwettbewerb wird nach
räumlichen Entwicklungsstrategien gesucht, um die «internationale Zone» zu
strukturieren und für Besucher attraktiver
zu gestalten. Das Programm umfasst Bauten für internationale Organisationen mit
einer Geschossfläche von über 60'000 m²,
die alle im Nahbereich der «Place des Nations» zu situieren sind. Unser Projekt
bringt eine Klärung und Präzisierung des
Ortes als Schnittstelle und Übergang vom
dichten Stadtgefüge zur «administrativen
Gartenstadt».

In this competition for ideas, spatial development strategies were sought in order
to structure the "international zone" and
to make it more attractive for visitors. The
program comprised buildings for international organizations with an overall floor
area of over 60,000m² that all had to be situated in the vicinity of the "Place des Nations." Our projects offered a clarification
and specification of the location as an in-
terface and transition from the dense urban structure to the "administrative garden city."

P: Kurt Aellen mit/with arb, A: Place des
Nations, Genève

Oberes Murifeld
1995–97 Renovation

Die über siebzigjährigen Wohnhäuser weisen einen ungenügenden Wohnkomfort auf. Aufgrund einer MieterInnen-Initiative wählt die Stadt für die Umbau- und Erneuerungsarbeiten einen neuen, unkonventionellen Weg: Die MieterInnen können mitbestimmen und mitwirken. Als Entscheidungshilfe dient ein Baukasten-Katalog mit allen möglichen wertvermehrenden Massnahmen und den entsprechenden Mietzinsaufschlägen. So können die MieterInnen den Komfort und die Miete selber beeinflussen.

The living comfort in the 70+-year-old apartment houses was inadequate. Due to an initiative by the tenants, the city selected an unconventional direction for the conversion and renewal work: the tenants were given a say and were able to make contributions. A modular system catalog with all kinds of value-increasing measures and the appropriate rent increases served as an aid for making decisions. The tenants could thus influence not only the comfort level but also the rent they would be paying for it.

P/R: arb, A: Kasthoferstrasse 4–8 und/ and 18, Bern

Haus Brunnadern
House Brunnadern
1991–93 Projekt/Project
1995–96 Bau/Construction

Das Wohnhaus mit Dienstleistungsbetrieben im Sockelgeschoss bildet zusammen mit dem Altbau (in dem sich unser Atelier befindet) den Abschluss einer Wohnzone. Ein öffentlicher Platz verbindet Neu- und Altbau zu einem Ensemble. Tiefe Ost-West-Grundrisse mit grosszügigen Nebenzonen kennzeichnen die durch drei Treppenhäuser erschlossenen Wohnungen des Neubaues. Abweichend von dieser Typologie sind die stirnseitigen Grundrisse im Volumen und der Raumorganisation auf Lage und Umgebung abgestimmt.

The apartment house, with service businesses on the first floor, forms the termination of an apartment zone together with the old structure (within which our studio is located). A public square connects the new and old building to create an ensemble. Deep east-west ground plans characterize the apartments of the new building, which are accessed via three staircases. As an exception to this typology, the ground plans in front, in their volume and spatial organization, are adjusted to the location and surroundings.

P/R: arb, A: Staufferstrasse 4–8, Bern

228

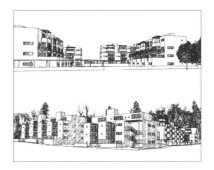

Anbau Haus Messerli
Addition House Messerli
1993 Projekt/Project
1994 Bau/Construction

Als Ersatz für die einsturzgefährdete Anlage in Mauerwerk- und Holzkonstruktion haben wir mit einem Gartensitzplatz, einer Pergola und einem überdeckten Balkon den Aussenraum des bestehenden Hauses räumlich gefasst und neu definiert. Die verwendeten Materialien Beton, verzinkter Stahl und Glas bilden einen gewollten Kontrast zur natürlichen Umgebung.

As a replacement for the dilapidated masonry and wood construction, we spatially held and redefined the outdoor space of the existing house with a garden patio, a pergola and a covered balcony. The materials used – concrete, galvanized steel and glass – form an intentional contrast with the natural surroundings.

P/R: arb, A: Kaufdorf, BE

Wohnbauten Biel-Madretsch
Apartment Buildings Biel-Madretsch
1994 Wettbewerb/Competition

Im Perimeter des Überbauungsplanes Madretsch-Ried sind am Siedlungsrand auf einem Areal von 1 ha preisgünstige Wohnungen zu planen. Die Überbauungsordnung gibt eine sehr eng gefasste Volumetrie vor. Die sich widersprechenden Forderungen nach optimal gegliedertem Bauvolumen einerseits und tiefen Erstellungskosten andererseits führen zu einem streng kubischen Gestaltungsprinzip das sowohl für die Ost-West als auch für die Nord-Süd orientierten Gebäude gilt.

In the perimeter of the development plan Madretsch-Ried, cost-efficient apartments needed to be planned at the edge of the development on a 1-hectare site. The development organization stipulated very tight volumetrics. The contradictory requests for optimally structured building volumes, on the one hand, and low construction costs, on the other, led to a strictly cubic design principle that applies to the buildings with an east-west orientation as well as those oriented north-south.

P: arb, A: Mösli-Quartier, Biel-Madretsch

Wohnbauten Freischützstrasse München
Apartment Buildings
Freischützstrasse München
1994 Wettbewerb/Competition

Zentrum Bahnhof Gümligen
Center Station Gümligen
1994 Wettbewerb/Competition

Auf einer noch offenen Teilfläche eines Wohngebietes der 60er Jahre sind Wohnbauten mit Geschosswohnungen zu projektieren. Sie sollen sich in den angrenzenden Grünbereich sensibel einfügen. Unser Projekt bringt das ganze Wohnprogramm in einem einzigen langen, auf Stützen gehobenen Baukörper unter. Durch die Schrägstellung des Gebäudes und durch die weitgehende Transparenz im Erdgeschoss werden Strassen und Parkräume miteinander verbunden und das Quartier mit dem stadtweit bedeutenden Grünzug vernetzt.

On an open site in a residential area from the sixties, apartment buildings with simple apartments needed to be designed. They were to be sensibly integrated into the adjoining green area. Our project contains the entire apartment program in a single, long, horizontal building volume raised up on supports. Due to the angled position of the building and the large degree of transparency on the first floor, streets and park spaces are interconnected and the quarter is networked with the green belt that is important for the whole city.

P: arb mit/with Franz Vogel, Bern,
A: Freischützstrasse, München

Gesucht sind Vorschläge für die planerische Festlegung und etappenweise Realisierung einer gesamtheitlichen Überbauung im Bereich des Bahnhofs Gümligen. Unser Projekt baut auf zwei gegensätzlichen Geometrien auf. Jener der Parzellenordnung und jener der Bahnlinie. Der Bahnhofplatz wird durch die beiden je einer Geometrie folgenden Hauptbaukörper gebildet. Das Entwicklungskonzept akzeptiert den durch die Eisenbahn erzeugten Einschnitt im Ortsbild. Der grosszügige Ausbau der bestehenden Unterführung löst das Dilemma.

Proposals for the planned determination and phased realization of an overall development in the area of the Gümligen station were wanted. Our project was based on two contrary geometrics: that of the parcel structure and that of the railroad tracks. The two main building volumes, each of which follows its own geometry, form the square of the station. The development concept accepts the incision in the district's appearance created by the railroad. The generous extension of the existing underpass solves the dilemma.

P: arb, A: Bahnhof Gümligen

Wohnprojekt Unterdettigen
Housing Project Unterdettigen
1993–94 Studie/Study

Schanzenpost
1986–87 Studien/Studies
1990–92 Projekt/Project
1993–1998 Bau/Construction

Direkt anschliessend an die Siedlung Hintere Aumatt sollen auf einem Areal von 2 ha weitere Wohnungen erstellt werden. Wir schlagen einen V-förmigen Gebäudewinkel vor. Die Öffnung des Winkels durch den zweiten Baukörper leitet den organischen Übergang zur Landschaft ein. Der sich ausweitende öffentliche Platz geht kontinuierlich in die Landschaft über. Ein zum bestehenden Siedlungsrand paralleler Baukörper stellt die architektonische Verbindung zur Hinteren Aumatt her.

Additional apartments were to be erected on a 2-hectare site directly adjoining the Hintere Aumatt development. We proposed a V-shaped angular building. The opening of the angle through the second building volume initiates the organic transition into the landscape. The expanding public square continuously merges with the landscape. A building volume placed parallel to the existing edge of the development creates the architectural connection.

P: arb, A: Aumatt, Hinterkappelen

Grundlagen für die Um- und Erweiterungsbauten sind eine Machbarkeitsstudie und eine neue Überbauungsordnung. Die baulichen Eingriffe betreffen den Gesamtkomplex der Schanzenpost. Im Ostteil der Anlage wird der über den Gleisen liegende langgezogene Baukörper der Briefämter saniert und durch Neubauten erweitert. Die Paket- und Briefämter werden umgebaut. Alle Publikumsräume, die Schalterhalle und die vorgelagerte Passage werden neu gestaltet.

The basis for the conversion and extension work was a feasibility study and a new superstructure regulation. The architectural interventions concern the overall Schanzenpost complex. On the east side of the complex, the long, horizontal building volume above the tracks housing the mail offices was redeveloped and extended with new buildings. The package and mail offices were converted. All public spaces, the counter hall and the passageway in front were redesigned.

P/R: arb, A: Schanzenstrasse 4, Bern

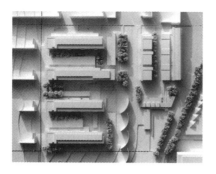

Brünnen Nord
1992 Wettbewerb/Competition

Eine Siedlungsfläche von 34 ha soll mit preisgünstigen Wohnungen für ca. 3000 Personen sowie Betriebsflächen für ca. 1000 Arbeitsplätze bebaut werden. Der Ortsteil soll autonom lebensfähig sein, sich aber auch zu einem noch unbekannten grösseren Ganzen entwickeln können. In einer ersten Etappe, sind 20'000 m² Bruttogeschossfläche zu projektieren. Unser Vorschlag basiert auf der Fortsetzung der städtebaulichen Identität von Bümpliz. Die «grüne Wiese» wird mit niedrigen Bauten belegt, so dass keine Einschränkungen für künftige Entwicklungen geschaffen werden.

An area of 34-hectares was to be developed with cost-efficient apartments for approximately 3,000 people and work spaces for approximately 1,000 jobs. The planned district was to be autonomously viable but also capable of developing as an element of a yet unknown, larger whole. In a first phase, a floor space of 20,000m² was to be planned. Our proposal was based on the continuation of the urban identity of Bümpliz. The undeveloped area is settled with low buildings, thus avoiding any limitations for future developments.

P: arb, A: Brünnen Nord, Bern

SRG und/and SRI
seit/since 1992 Um- und Anbauten/
Conversions and Extensions

Die Generaldirektion der Schweizerischen Radio- und Fernsehgesellschaft SRG und das Schweizer Radio International SRI belegen zwei Gebäude im Berner Ostring. Das übergeordnete Ziel aller Interventionen ist, den Gebäuden eine Identität zu geben, die der Bedeutung dieser Unternehmen entspricht. Zwei Restaurants werden umgebaut. Die Direktionsetage wird repräsentativ gestaltet. Das Gebäude Giacomettistrasse 1 wird mit Büro- und Redaktionsräumen sowie Sendestudios für fremdsprachige Ketten umgebaut.

The general direction of the Swiss Radio and TV Society and the Swiss Radio International occupy two buildings. The goal of all interventions is to provide buildings with identities that reflect the importance of the enterprises. Two restaurants were converted. The floor with the offices of the direction is designed in a representative fashion. The building at Giacomettistrasse 1 was converted with office and editing rooms as well as studios for foreign-language broadcasting.

P/R: arb mit/with Kathrin Eichenberger
A: Giacomettistrasse 1 und/and 3, Bern

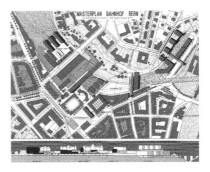

BFF-Schule Bern
BFF School Bern
1992 Studie/Study
1992–2000 Bau/Construction

Der Raumbestand und die Nutzung der Be-
rufs-, Fach- und Fortbildungsschule (BFF)
haben sich in den Jahren vor 1992 eher zufällig entwickelt. Die Räumlichkeiten sind
über mehrere Häuser der Jahrhundertwen-
de verstreut. Bei der Sanierung und dem
Umbau realisieren wir ein Konzept, das einerseits die Nutzungsoptimierung und andererseits eine umfassende, Identität ver-
mittelnde Gestaltung in den Vordergrund
stellt. Der Eindruck einer Gesamtschule
wird betont, ohne dass dabei die einzelnen
Abteilungen ihr Eigenleben verlieren.

The existing space and use of the Voca-
tional, Technical and Continuing Education
School (BFF) had developed in a rather arbitrary way before 1992. The rooms are
spread throughout several turn-of-the-cen-
tury buildings. During the redevelopment
and conversion, we realized a concept,
which on one hand emphasizes the optimization of the use and, on the other, a
comprehensive design that communicates
an identity. The impression of a comprehensive school is strengthened without the
individual departments losing the life of
their own.

P/R: arb, Künstler/Artist: Hanswalter Graf,
A: Monbijou- und/and Kapellenstrasse,
Bern

Masterplan Bahnhof Bern
Master Plan Bern Station
1992–93 Planung/Plan

Für die Umgestaltung des Bahnhofs ist der
Projektkommission für den Bereich Städtebau eine Begleitgruppe zur Seite gestellt.
Anknüpfend an unsere Studie von 1989 bearbeiten wir den Baustein Umsteigeplatt-
form über den Gleisen auf der Westseite
und den Baustein Lange Schanze, der auf
die unbefriedigende städtebauliche Situation des westlichen Abschlusses der Perronplatte reagiert. Diese Vorarbeiten führen zu den vom Volk genehmigten Nut-
zungsplänen, Basis für kommende Archi-
tekturwettbewerbe.

The project commission, Master Plan, for
the field of urbanism had an accompanying
group by its side for the redesign of the
Bern station. Connecting with our 1989
study, we worked on the platform element
above the tracks on the west side and the
Lange Schanze element, which reacts to the
unsatisfactory urban situation of the west-
ern termination, the Perronplatte. This preliminary work led to the utilization plans
agreed to by the people involved, the basis for any future architectural competi-
tions.

P: Kurt Aellen mit/with Alfredo Pini,
Pierre Clemençon, Rudolf Rast
(Coordinator), A: Bahnhof Bern

Bundeshauserweiterung
Bundeshaus Extension
1991 Studie/Study

Esslinger Dreieck
Esslingen Triangle
1990 Wettbewerb/Competition

Machbarkeitsstudien sollen aufzeigen, wie der Raumbedarf des Parlaments befriedigt werden kann. Das Thema der Verbindung vom Fluss zum Stadtkörper auf der Hangkante, mit den historischen Wegen, Treppen und Stützmauern, wird von uns neu formuliert. Der filigrane Turm des Medienzentrums, der langgestreckte Terrassenbau mit den Parlamentsdiensten, das in Schichten gegliederte Hauptgebäude der Parlamentarier, die erweiterte Bundesterrasse und die Bundeshausbauten bilden eine neue städtebauliche Einheit.

Feasibility studies were to show how the spatial needs of the parliament could be satisfied. The theme of connecting the river and the section of the city, lying at the edge of the hillside with the historic pathways, stairs and reinforcing walls was reformulated by us. The filigree tower of the media center, the long, horizontal terrace building with the parliament services, the main buildings of the parliamentarians structured in layers, the extended federal terrace and the Bundeshaus buildings form a new urban unity.

P: arb, A: Parlamentsgebäude, Bern

In Esslingen, einem Vorort von Zürich, bietet sich durch die Verlegung des Bahnhofs die Möglichkeit, das Zentrum neu zu gestalten. Unser Projekt fasst die gesamte Baumasse in einem engen Bereich zusammen. Durch diese Konzentration aller Aktivitäten und Verkehrswege entsteht ein wirkliches Zentrum. Die markante Struktur des Landschaftsraumes wird vom neuen Quartier übernommen und fortgesetzt. Gleichzeitig zeigen wir wünschenswerte Entwicklungen für die Nachbargrundstücke auf.

In Esslingen, a suburb of Zurich, the transfer of the station offered the opportunity to redesign the center. Our project combined the entire building mass in a narrow area. This concentration of all activities and traffic routes creates a true center. The striking structure of the landscaped space is adopted and continued by the new quarter. At the same time we point out desirable developments for the neighboring properties.

P: arb, A: Endstation Forchbahn, Esslingen

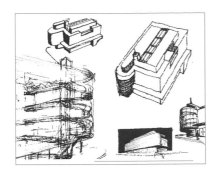 

Geschäftshaus Warth
Business Building Warth
1989–1990 Projekt/Project

Tramdepot Saali
Tram Depot Saali
1989–1991 Studien/Studies

Das Grundstück Warth liegt an einem markanten Ort in Rapperswil, an der Pforte zur Altstadt und am Nadelöhr der berüchtigten Hauptverkehrsader über den Zürichseedamm. Mit einem Neubau kann der Ort städtebaulich aufgewertet und besser genutzt werden. Wir schlagen einen einfachen Baukörper vor, der im Innern einen möglichst hohen Erlebniswert aufweist. Das Gebäude ist vom Dach bis ins Erdgeschoss aufgeschnitten. So entsteht räumliche Transparenz, die über das innere Wegnetz erlebt werden kann.

The Warth site is located at a prominent place in Rapperswil, the gate to the old part of town and the bottleneck of the infamous main traffic vein across Zürichseedamm. The site can be increased in value in an urban sense and better utilized with a new building. We suggested a simple building volume that offers a level of experience inside that is as high as possible. The building is cut open from the roof to the first floor. This creates a spatial transparency that can be experienced beyond the network of walkways inside.

P: arb, A: Cityplatz, Rapperswil am Zürichsee

Der Spielraum für die künftige Entwicklung der Städtischen Verkehrsbetriebe Bern wird ausgeleuchtet und die Standortfragen der Werkanlagen untersucht. Unsere Machbarkeitsstudie zeigt, dass am östlichen Stadtrand ein Depot möglich ist. Eine erweiterte städtebauliche Entwicklungsstudie zeigt ausserdem die Möglichkeit für eine mit Drittnutzungen kombinierte Werkanlage. Gleichzeitig legen wir dar, dass durch eine Verdichtung die Lärmemissionen der Autobahn unterbunden und das Wittigkofenquartier aufgewertet werden kann.

The elbowroom for the future development of the urban transport services in Bern was illuminated and questions regarding the location of the facility complexes were examined. Our feasibility study revealed that a depot was possible at the eastern edge of Bern. An extended urban development study additionally revealed the possibility for a facility complex combined with third-party users. We explained that by condensing this zone the noise emissions from the autobahn could be stopped and that the value of the Wittigkofen quarter could thus be increased.

P: arb mit/with Planconsult, Basel,
A: Wittigkofen, Bern

235

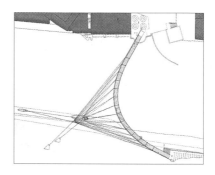

Steinhof Burgdorf
1989 Wettbewerb/Competition

Mattesteg
1989 Wettbewerb/Competition

Das Lagerhausareal Steinhof wird neu hauptsächlich der Wohnnutzung zugeordnet, mit einem Gewerbebereich längs der Bahn. Die Schutzwürdigkeit der Brauereibauten wird durch den Erhalt des Hauptgebäudes und der Halle respektiert. Ein parallel zur Bahn gestellter Baukörper mit gemischter Nutzung dient als Lärmriegel. Bei der Stellung der dahinterliegenden Wohnbauten nehmen wir auf die Gewölbekeller Rücksicht und schaffen mittels präziser Anordnung und Terrassierung eine Folge von aufeinander abgestimmten Aussenräumen.

The storage house area Steinhof is redesigned mainly for residential purposes, with an industrial area along the railroad tracks. The historic protection of the brewery buildings is respected by preserving the main building and the hall behind it. A building volume with a mixed use placed parallel to the railroad tracks serves as a noise barrier. In the positioning of the apartment buildings behind it, we considered the vaulted cellars and created a sequence of harmonic outdoor spaces through their precise arrangement and through terracing.

P: arb, A: Areal Steinhof, Burgdorf

Bei unserem Projekt geht es nicht einfach darum, die Aare auf dem kürzesten Weg zu überqueren, sondern um das Erlebnis des Überschreitens des Flusses. Unser Steg führt geschwungen erst gegen, dann mit der Strömung über die Aare. So werden die Ufer auf eine an sich natürliche Weise verlassen und wieder erreicht. Wie ein Boot stösst der Fussgänger vom Ufer ab und legt am anderen Ufer wieder an.

Our project not only dealt with simply crossing the Aare river in the shortest possible way but also with the experience of walking across the river. Our footbridge first curves against the current and then with it as it crosses the Aare. The banks are thus left behind and then approached again in a natural way. Like a boat, the pedestrian pushes of the bank and goes ashore on the other side.

P: arb, A: Wasserwerkgasse, Bern

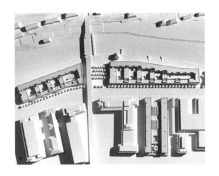

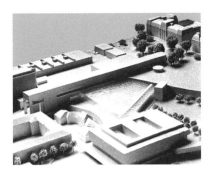

Fabrikgelände Hardturmstrasse
Factory Grounds Hardturmstrasse
1989 Wettbewerb/Competition

Studie Bahnhof Bern
Study Bern Station
1989 Wettbewerb/Competition

Die bestehende Bebauung nördlich und südlich der Hardturmstrasse soll durch neue Wohn-, Gewerbe- und Dienstleistungsbauten mit ca. 47'000 m² Nutzflächen ersetzt werden. Das Projekt soll der speziellen Lage zwischen der Einfallsachse und dem landschaftlich schönen Limmatraum gerecht werden. Unser Vorschlag ist eine Kasbah-ähnliche Bebauung längs der Limmat. Dank verdichteter Bauweise gelingt es, im Bereich des trennenden SBB-Viadukts einen grosszügigen Platz zu schaffen und den Blick auf den Hardturm offenzulegen.

The existing superstructures north and south of Hardturmstrasse were to be replaced with new apartment, business and service buildings with a floor space of approximately 47,000m². The project was to do justice to the special situation between the access axis and the beautiful landscape around the Limmat. Our proposal is a Kasbah-like superstructure along the river. Due to a condensed building style, we succeeded in creating a generous square in the area of the separating railroad viaduct and to open up the view towards Hardturm.

P: arb, A: Hardturmstrasse, Zürich

Der Mitte der siebziger Jahre fertiggestellte Bahnhof von Bern soll umgebaut werden. Keine grossen Würfe sind gefragt, sondern eine Situationsreparatur. Kernpunkte unseres zur Überarbeitung empfohlenen Projektes sind der Neubau der «Langen Schanze» und ein zweiter Bahnhofplatz auf der Ebene Busbahnhof. Mit der Verbesserung der Fussgängerverbindungen und mit Nutzungsverdichtungen wird eine räumliche Klärung erreicht. Der zweite Bahnhofplatz ist ein wichtiges Element im Stadtraum. Auch im Hinblick auf kommende Gleisüberbauungen.

The station in Bern that was completed in the mid-seventies was to be converted. The competition did not call for a great strike but rather merely a repair of the situation. The main points of our project recommended for the conversion were the construction of the "Lange Schanze" and a second station square on the level of the bus terminal. With the improvement of the pedestrian connections and the condensation of the utilization a spatial clarification was achieved. The second station square is an essential element in the urban space with respect to future track superstructures as well.

P: arb, A: Bahnhof Bern

237

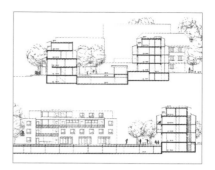

Wohnbauten Vermontpark
Apartment Buildings Vermontpark
1983 Wettbewerb/Competition
1988–90 Bau/Construction

In einem alten, zum Teil bewaldeten Park
im Osten der Stadt Bern werden im Projekt
vier Wohnbauten so angeordnet, dass die
markante, Räume bildende Bepflanzung erhalten bleibt. Die unterschiedlich grossen
Wohnungen in den beiden realisierten Gebäuden der ersten Etappe besitzen alle Terrassen, welche der aussergewöhnlich at-
traktiven Wohnlage im Vermontpark Rechnung tragen.

In an old, partially wooded park on the east
side of the city of Bern, four apartment
buildings were arranged in the plan in a
way that allowed the striking, space-creat-
ing plantings to be preserved. The apartments of different sizes in the two buildings erected during the first phase all have
terraces that take the unusually attractive
location in Vermontpark into account.

P/R: arb, A: Buristrasse 9–17, Bern

Planungsviereck Lorraine
Plan Quadrangle Lorraine
1988 Wettbewerb/Competition

Das Planungsviereck liegt im Bereich des
Schutzplanes Lorraine. Die bestehende
Bausubstanz ist von unterschiedlicher Qualität, einige Gebäude sind in schlechtem
Zustand. Das Viereck soll mit Neu- und Um-
bauten nutzungsmässig und städtebaulich
aufgewertet werden. Unser Vorschlag übernimmt die offene Bauweise und gliedert
den Hofraum durch Nebenbauten und klare Nutzungszuweisungen. Das quer zur Lorrainestrasse stehende Gebäude wird mit
der strassenbegleitenden Baumreihe erhalten. Dieser räumliche Akzent wird zu einem Quartiermerkmal.

The quadrangle is located in the area of the
Lorraine protection plan. The existing
building substance was of varying quality;
some buildings were in bad condition. The
quadrangle was to be upgraded with new
buildings and conversions in a utilitarian
and urban sense. Our proposal adopted the
open building style and structured the
courtyard space through side buildings and
clear purposes of use. The building placed
at a right angle to Lorrainstrasse, together
with the row of trees along the street, was
preserved. This spatial accentuation becomes a trademark for the quarter.

P: arb, A: Lorrainestrasse, Bern

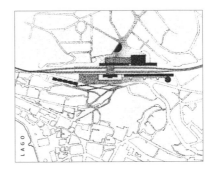

Wohnbauten St. Légier
Apartment Buildings in St Légier
1988 Wettbewerb/Competition

Bahnhof Lugano
Lugano Station
1987 Wettbewerb/Competition

Auf einer Parzelle von etwas mehr als 2 ha, die zum Teil durch Treibhäuser belegt ist, soll angrenzend an freistehende Einfamilienhäuser ein verdichteter Siedlungsteil entstehen. Bei unserem Vorschlag wird ein Teil der Glashäuser erhalten und umgenutzt, um die Identität des Ortes zu wahren. Gleichzeitig werden die erhaltenen Bauten zum Bindeglied zwischen den Reihenhäusern am Hang und jenen im flachen Teil des Areals.

On a parcel that is a little larger than 2 hectares and partially occupied by greenhouses, a condensed development was to be created aside from freestanding single-family homes. Sections of the greenhouses were converted in our proposal in order to preserve the identity of the site. At the same time, the preserved buildings would become a link between the row houses on the hill and those on the flat part of the grounds.

P: arb, A: Les Oches, St. Légier

Mit der Restrukturierung des Bahnhofareals soll die städtebauliche Bedeutung dieses Knotenpunktes verschiedener Verkehrsträger unterstrichen werden. Der gegebene Perimeter greift weit über den Bahnhof hinaus. Unser Projekt macht den Platz vor dem Bahnhof zur Aussichtsterrasse und schafft eine räumliche Verbindung durch den Bahnhof hindurch zu einem dahinterliegenden zweiten Platz. Dadurch wird dem bei Durchgangsbahnhöfen typischen Zerschneiden von Stadtteilen entgegengewirkt.

The redesign of the station area was to emphasize the urban importance of this junction point of various traffic carriers. The given perimeter went far beyond the station. Our project turned the square in front of the station into an observation terrace and created a spatial connection through the station to the second square behind it. This counteracts the separation of urban quarters typical in the case of transit stations.

P: arb, A: Bahnhof Lugano

Fernmeldedirektion Bern
Telecommunications Direction Bern
1980 Wettbewerb/Competition
1986–92 Bau/Construction

Auf einer von drei Verkehrsadern umfassten Parzelle werden als Ergänzung zur 1952 erbauten Fernmeldedirektion zwei neue Bürogebäude, ein Konferenztrakt und ein Mehrfamilienhaus erstellt. Unsere Neubauten sind auf das Quartierbild mit seinen klar definierten Strassenräumen abgestimmt. Als städtebaulicher Beitrag wird der Brunnhofweg wieder geöffnet. Dies ist möglich, weil wir den Konferenztrakt auf Säulen stellen. Der Bau von 1952 wird renoviert und das Innere dem Standard der Neubauten angepasst.

On a parcel surrounded by three traffic veins, two new office buildings, a conference tract and an apartment building for several families were added to the telecommunications direction building that dates back to 1952. Our new buildings are adapted to the quarter with its clearly defined street spaces. As an urban contribution, Brunnhofweg was reopened. This became possible because we placed the conference tract onto columns. The 1952 structure was renovated and the inside was adapted to the standards of the new buildings.

P/R: arb, A: Belpstrasse 48, Bern

Schweizerisches Paraplegiker-Zentrum
Swiss Paraplegics Center
1985 Wettbewerb/Competition

In Nottwil wird ein neues Zentrum aufgebaut für die Akutphase und die Erstrehabilitation Querschnittgelähmter. Unser Projekt konzentriert alle die Behinderung betreffenden Bereiche vom Akutspital bis zu Rehabilitation, Sport und Schulung und schafft dadurch eine Atmosphäre der Zuversicht. Durch visuelle Transparenz längs der Hauptachse, dem Rückgrat der Anlage, wird die vertikale Dimension trotz der verlorenen Beweglichkeit der Patienten erlebbar. Die Verkehrswege werden zu Erlebnisbereichen.

A new center is built in Nottwil for the critical phase and initial rehabilitation of paraplegics. Our project concentrated all areas concerning this handicap, from the intensive care hospital to rehabilitation, sports and education and thus creates an atmosphere of confidence. Given the visual transparency along the main axis, the backbone of the complex, the vertical dimension becomes tangible, despite the lost abilities of the patients to move freely on their own. The traffic routes become areas of experience.

P: arb, A: Nottwil

Umbau Nationalbank Bern
Conversion Nationalbank Bern
1982 Planung/Plan
1983–85 Bau/Construction

Der Umbau des 1909–11 erstellten Gebäudes betrifft ausschliesslich das Innere. Die Räume unter der Amthausgasse werden für die Unterbringung der EDV-Anlage ausgebaut. Die teilweise zerstörten Qualitäten des Gebäudes werden in Zusammenarbeit mit der Denkmalpflege zurückgewonnen und der Bau den künftigen Nutzungsbedürfnissen angepasst. Die komplexen Umbauarbeiten werden im gegebenen Kostenrahmen bei minimaler Störung des Betriebes realisiert.

The conversion of the building erected between 1909 and 1911 applies only to the interior. The spaces below Amthausgasse were extended in order to accommodate the computer system. The partially demolished qualities of the building were regained in line with the preservation of historic buildings and, simultaneously, the building was adjusted to meet the needs of future utilization. The complex conversion work was realized within the given budget and interfered only minimally with ongoing business.

P/R: arb mit/with Robert und Trix Haussmann, Zürich, A: Bundesplatz, Bern

Frauenspital Bern
Women's Hospital Bern
1983 Wettbewerb/Competition

Das heutige Frauenspital genügt den Anforderungen in baulicher und betrieblicher Hinsicht nicht mehr. Es wird deshalb an einem neuen Standort errichtet. Unser Projekt basiert auf einer einfach lesbaren, rationellen Baustruktur mit vielseitig verflochtenen innen- und aussenräumlichen Erlebnisbereichen: Park, Stadtbach, Eingangsgalerie, Dachterrasse, öffentlicher Durchgang. Trotz Nutzungsneutralität ist die Möglichkeit zur Entflechtung der einzelnen Betriebsbereiche gegeben.

The women's hospital was no longer able to fulfill its requirements in architectural and professional terms. Therefore, it was constructed in a new location. Our project was based on a simply legible, rational building structure with variably interwoven interior and outdoor areas of experience: park, city stream, entrance gallery, roof terrace, public passageway. Despite the neutrality of use, the possibility of unfolding the individual internal areas is a given.

P: arb mit/with Chi-Chen und Anton Herrmann-Chong, A: Effingerstrasse, Bern

Siedlung Merzenacker
Development Merzenacker
1974 Planungsbeginn/Planning Start
1983–87 Bau/Construction

Siedlung Hintere Aumatt
Development Hintere Aumatt
1973 Planungsbeginn/Planning Start
1981–92 Bau/Construction

Der Ausgleich zwischen individuellen Wohnbedürfnissen und dem Anspruch an die Gestaltung als eine Einheit prägt den Merzenacker. Die abgestufte und gegliederte Abfolge klar strukturierter Aussenräume führt zu räumlicher Kontinuität innerhalb der Siedlung. Das eigenständige Bebauungsmuster nimmt Bezug zu benachbarten Bauten und zur Landschaft. Mehrschichtig wie die gesamte Anlage ist auch die Struktur der einzelnen Häuser mit natürlich belichteten Innenzonen und Vorbauten, die den Übergang von innen nach aussen als Zwischenzone ausbilden.

The balance between individual living standards and the aim of design as an entity influenced Merzenacker. The stepped and arranged sequence of clearly structured outdoor spaces creates a spatial continuity within the development. The independent pattern of development relates to the neighboring buildings and the landscape. The structure of the individual houses, like the complex as a whole, has multiple layers with naturally lit interior zones and porches that form the transition between inside and outside as an interim zone.

P/R: arb, A: Merzenacker, Bern

Wir ordnen Wohn- und Atelierbauten in Bauzeilen so an, dass zwischen den parallelen Gebäudereihen eine Raumfolge von Gassen, Plätzen und Durchgängen entsteht. An diesem öffentlichen Aussenraum liegen hangseitig im Sockel der Wohngebäude Ateliers und Gemeinschaftsräume. Auf der gegenüberliegenden Seite bilden die Vorgärten der Reihenhäuser einen Filter zwischen privatem Wohnbereich und öffentlicher Gasse. Das enge urbane Gefüge bildet einen beabsichtigten Kontrast zur ländlichen Umgebung.

We arranged apartment and studio buildings in rows so as to cause a spatial sequence of alleys, squares and passageways to emerge between the parallel rows of buildings. In the base level of the apartment buildings, studios and communal rooms are situated on the side facing the slope, oriented towards this public outdoor space. On the opposite side, the small gardens in front of the row houses form a kind of filter between the private living area and the public alley. The dense urban network creates an intentional contrast with the rural surroundings.

P/R: arb, Bepflanzungkonzept/Landscaping concept: Arthur Kirchhofer, Therese Lindt Kirchhofer, Gümmenen, A: Hinterkappelen

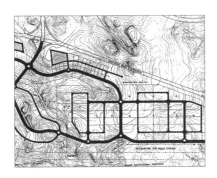

Industriegebiet Abuja
Industrial Area Abuja
1981 Planung/Plan

Pachtgut Bannholz
Lease Farm Bannholz
1979 Wettbewerb/Competition
1981–82 Bau/Construction

Die neue Hauptstadt Nigerias, Abuja, soll bis ins Jahr 2000 drei Millionen Einwohner beherbergen. Die Planung von zwei Industriezonen und einem Wohngebiet, wird einem internationalen Konsortium übertragen. Unsere Aufgabe besteht in der Planung der Ansiedlung von umweltverträglichen Industrien und zugeordneten Ausbildungsstätten. Die Resultate sind Nutzungszonen-, Infrastruktur- und Etappierungspläne, begleitet von einem umfassenden Bericht mit Vorschlägen, wie das Industriegebiet in offener Planung schrittweise realisiert werden kann.

Abuja, the new capital of Nigeria, wanted to offer homes to three million inhabitants by the year 2000. The planning of two industrial areas and a residential area was assigned to an international consortium. Our task consisted of planning the settlement of environmentally friendly industries and the appropriate educational centers. The results were plans for utilization zones, infrastructure and phases, accompanied by a comprehensive report with proposals on how the industrial area can be realized step-by-step in an open plan.

P: arb mit/with Planconsult Basel
A: Abuja, Nigeria

Der Neubau des kantonalen Pachtgutes ist uns Anlass für die neuzeitliche Organisation eines Bauernhofes. Der Bau vereinigt unter einem grossen Dach sämtliche Betriebsräume – Boxenlaufstall, Kälber- und Jungviehställe und Pferdestall. Eine Ebene tiefer liegen die Maschinenhalle, Lagerräume, Fahrzeuggarage und Werkstatt. Die Wohnnutzungen sind in einem separaten Gebäude untergebracht. Der Vorbildcharakter des Betriebs wird durch die Biogasanlage unterstrichen.

The new construction of the cantonal lease farm was an occasion for us to organize a farm in a contemporary manner. Beneath a large roof that follows the hillside situation, the building unites all of the facilities – box stable, calf and young cattle stables and horse stable. The machine hall, storage rooms, vehicle garage and workshop are one level below; the apartments are located in a separate building. The exemplary character of the business is emphasized through the biogas system.

P/R: Martin Wyss mit/with arb, A: Köniz

Alterspflegeheim Steffisburg
Seniors Nursing Home Steffisburg
1980 Wettbewerb/Competition

Für pflegebedürftige Menschen ein Heim zu bauen, in dem sie den Lebensabend verbringen, verlangt Einfühlungsvermögen. Die wohnliche Atmosphäre unseres Projektes hebt das Wohlbefinden der Bewohner. Im ausgesprochen niedrigen Baukörper mit zwei grossen Innenhöfen liegen die meisten Räume und Raumverbindungen an einer Fassade. Licht tritt aus verschiedenen Himmelsrichtungen ins Gebäude ein. Anstelle der üblichen monotonen Spitalzimmer schlagen wir Räume vor mit unterschiedlichen Zonen, Ausblicken und Lichteinfällen.

Building a home for people in need of care to spend their old age requires a great deal of empathy. The cozy atmosphere of our project increases the well-being of the inhabitants. In the decidedly low building volume with two large inner courtyards, most rooms and spatial connections are situated at a façade. Natural light enters the building from different directions. Instead of the normally monotonous hospital rooms, we suggest rooms with different zones, views and light incidences.

P: arb, A: Ziegeleistrasse, Steffisburg

Käfigturm
1980 Studie/Study

Ausgangspunkt ist ein Eingriff, der im frühen 19. Jahrhundert eine Lücke zwischen Käfigturm und angrenzenden Gebäuden hinterlassen hat. Unser Projekt schliesst diese Lücke und trennt die Zonen für die Strassenbahn und die Fussgänger. Die Fussgänger werden neu, in der verlängerten Achse der Marktgasslaube, unter der Häuserzeile hindurch auf den Waisenhausplatz geführt. Mit Treppe und Lift wird der Zugang zum Käfigturm verbessert und gleichzeitig werden die Terrassen der Häuser am Waisenhausplatz erschlossen.

The starting point was an intervention that left a gap between the Käfigturm and the adjoining buildings in the 19th century. Our project closed this gap and separated the zone for the tram and the pedestrians. The pedestrians are guided in a new way, in the extended axis of Marktgasslaube, beneath the row of houses to Waisenhausplatz. With stairs and elevator, the access to Käfigturm is improved and, simultaneously, the terraces of the houses at Waisenhausplatz are developed.

P: arb, A: Käfigturm, Bern

Schulheim Schloss Erlach
School Hostel Erlach Castle
1975 Wettbewerb/Competition
1980–84 Bau/Construction

Beim Ausbau und der Umwandlung der
Bauten in ein Schulheim gilt es, gute Vor-
aussetzungen für den Betrieb zu schaffen
und die historisch wertvolle Bausubstanz
zu respektieren. Vier Wohngruppen sind in
den Altstadthäusern und im neuen Zwischenbau untergebracht. Schulbetrieb und
Turnhalle befinden sich im Konviktgebäude. Das gewählte Pavillonsystem wird den
erzieherischen Aufgaben optimal gerecht.

During the extension and conversion of the
buildings into a school hostel, the point
was to create proper preconditions for the
utilization and to respect the historically
precious building substance. Four community spaces are housed in the old town
houses and the new building between. The
classrooms and gymnasium are located in
the hostel building. The pavilion system
does justice to the educational tasks in an
optimal way.

P: arb mit/with Daniel Reist, R: arb,
A: Schloss Erlach

Mufindi Township
1978–80 Planung/Plan

Auf Tanzanias Weg zur industriellen De-
zentralisierung werden neue Werke in in-
dustriearmen Regionen angesiedelt. Mufindi ist für eine Papierfabrik und eine zu-
geordnete Siedlung mit 10'000 Einwohnern
vorgesehen. Wir erarbeiten Nutzungs- und
Infrastrukturpläne, Entwurfsrichtlinien und
Vorschläge zu Wachstum und Verdichtung.
Die Infrastruktur ist von einem Bebauungsmuster überlagert. Dabei ist ein Sektor für
«sites and services» reserviert, wo wir im
Hinblick auf Selbstbau der Bewohner nur
die Hausanschlüsse vorsehen.

On Tanzania's path towards industrial de-
centralization, new factories were being
settled in regions with little or no industry.
Mufindi was designated for a paper factory and housing development for 10,000 inhabitants. We developed utilization and infrastructure plans, which we complemented with design guidelines and proposals on
growth and condensation. One sector was
reserved for sites and services where, with
respect to the construction by the inhabitants, we only planned for the branch lines
to the buildings.

P: Planconsult Basel mit/with arb, O-Con-
sult, Offenbach, Pierre Gurtner und Walter
Lang, Lausanne, A: bei/near Iringa, Tanzania

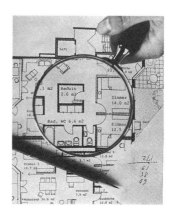

Sanitätspolizei
1977 Planung/Plan
1978–81 Bau/Construction

Die Sanitätspolizei wird in ein schützens-
wertes Gebäude, das frühere «Freie Gymnasium» in der Stadtmitte von Bern, ver-
legt. Die Integration der Garage in die gegebene Baustruktur führt zwangsläufig zur
völligen Auskernung des Gebäudes bis zur
Decke des ersten Obergeschosses. Die
schweren Sandsteinwände müssen durch
stockwerkhohe Stahlfachwerke abgefan-
gen werden. Die in die Fassadengeometrie
eingefügte sichtbare Stahlkonstruktion
fasst die Garagentore und die Fenster des
Zwischengeschosses zusammen.

The Sanitätspolizei was moved into a building, the former "Freies Gymnasium" that is
worth preserving in the center of Bern. The
integration of the garage into the existing
building structure necessarily led to the
complete removal of the installations inside the building up to the ceiling of the
second floor. The heavy limestone walls
had to be supported by floor-height steel
framework. The visible steel construction
integrated into the geometry of the façade
unites the garage doors and windows of the
mezzanine.

P/R: arb mit/with Daniel Reist und Alfred
Vollenwyder, A: Nägeligasse 2, Prediger-
gasse 12, Bern

Wohnungs-Bewertungs-System (WBS)
Apartment Evaluation System (WBS)
1975 Erstausgabe/First Edition
1986 2. Ausgabe/2nd Edition
2000 3. Ausgabe/3rd Edition

Das WBS dient dem Bundesamt für Woh-
nungswesen zur Ermittlung des Gebrauchs-
wertes einer Wohnung und als Entscheidungshilfe bei der Beurteilung der Förde-
rungswürdigkeit. Die Merkmale des zu be-
wertenden Wohnbaus können entsprechend
den Präferenzen der Benutzer in einem Ge-
samtmass erfasst werden. Die seit 1975
durchgeführten Messungen wurden 1979
statistisch ausgewertet. Wie beabsichtigt,
kann das offene System aufgrund der Erfahrungen in der Anwendung laufend angepasst und verbessert werden.

The WBS aids the Federal Housing Office in
assessing apartment values and as a deci-
sion-making aid for evaluating sponsor-
ship. The characteristics of the apartment
building being evaluated can be recorded,
according to the preferences of the users,
in an overall assessment. The value as-
sessments made since 1975 were statisti-
cally exploited in 1979. As intended, the
open system can be constantly adjusted
and improved as a result of the experiences
gained through its practical application.

Verfasser/Authors: Kurt Aellen, Thomas
Keller, Paul Meyer, Jürgen Wiegand

Schul- und Kirchgemeindezentrum
School and Church Community Center
1972 Wettbewerb/Competition
1973–75 Bau/Construction

Das Schulhaus in Neuenegg-Dorf soll zu einem Schulzentrum mit Primar- und Sekundarschule, Sportanlagen und Einrichtungen für die Kirchgemeinde erweitert werden. Die gebaute erste Etappe fasst die Sekundarschule und die Räumlichkeiten der Kirchgemeinde zu einer Einheit zusammen. Vom bewährten Bausystem CROCS übernehmen wir den Stahlbau. Um einen individuellen Ausdruck zu erreichen, werden CROCS-Bauteile speziell für diesen Bau weiterentwickelt.

The schoolhouse in Neuenegg-Dorf was to be extended into a school center, with a primary and secondary school, sports facilities and rooms for the church community. The realized first phase unites the secondary school and the rooms of the church community. We adopted the steel construction from the proven building system CROCS. In order to achieve an individual appearance, CROCS components were developed especially for this building.

P/R: arb mit/with Kurt Aellen, Franz Biffiger, Daniel Reist, Bernhard Suter, Künstler/artist: Ueli Berger, A: Schulhausstrasse, Neuenegg

Kindergarten Seidenberg
1973 Projekt und Bau/Project and
Construction

Der Kindergarten für eine einzige Klasse wird auf die Decke einer unterirdischen Einstellhalle mitten in ein bestehendes Wohnquartier gestellt. Der eingeschossige Baukörper ist eine leichte Holzständerkonstruktion, gefalzte, geschosshohe Aluminiumbleche bilden die Aussenhaut. Der Grundriss gleicht einem Schneckenhaus in das man sich zurückziehen kann. Alle Räume – Eingang, Garderobe, Arbeitsraum, Küche, WC und der Hauptraum – drehen sich um eine kleine Oberlichtgalerie. Einzig der Hauptraum hat eine grosszügige Öffnung zum Aussenraum.

The kindergarten for a single class was placed on top of a subterranean parking garage in the middle of an existing quarter. The one-story building volume is a light post-and-beam construction. Folded floor-to-ceiling aluminum sheet metal forms the outer shell. The ground plan resembles a snail shell into which one can withdraw. All rooms – entrance, wardrobe, office, kitchen, bathroom and the main room – revolve around a small skylit gallery. Only the main room has a generous opening towards the outside space.

P: Daniel Reist, R: arb, A: Beethovenstrasse 17, Gümligen

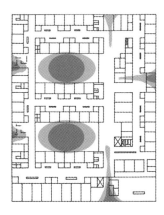

Turm auf dem Ulmizberg
Tower on Ulmizberg
1970 Wettbewerb/Competition
1972–75 Bau/Construction

Entgegen den Vorgaben setzen wir den
Standort des Turmes an die Hangkante und
wählen anstelle von Beton eine transparente, windsteife Stahlkonstruktion. So stö-
ren wir die Silhouette des Waldes nicht und
lösen die Aufgabe mit geringerer Bauhöhe.
Der weltweit erste Richtstrahlantennen-
Träger aus Stahl ist das Resultat der intensiven Auseinandersetzung mit einem ex-
ponierten Ort.

Contrary to the conditions stipulated by the
competition, we moved the location of the
tower to the edge of the hill and chose a
transparent, wind-braced steel construction instead of concrete. Thus, we don't dis-
turb the silhouette of the forest, and solve
the task with a lower building height. The
first directional antennae tower in the
world that is made of steel is the result of
an intense confrontation with an exposed
site.

P/R: arb mit/with Kurt Aellen,
Franz Biffiger, Urs Hettich, Daniel Reist,
Bernhard Suter, Fassadenkonzept/
façade-concept: Jean Prouvé, Paris,
A: Ulmizberg, Köniz

Spital Münsingen
Hospital Münsingen
1972 Wettbewerb/Competition

Wir gehen davon aus, dass der Flächenbe-
darf des Behandlungsbereiches im Verhält-
nis zum Pflegebereich zunehmen wird. Deshalb schlagen wir einen zwei- bis dreige-
schossigen Flachbau vor, der spätere Ver-
schiebungen einzelner Bereiche erleichtert.
Die damals gängige Trennung von Pflege-
einheit und Behandlungstrakt lehnen wir
ab. Gezielte Ausblicke in die Weite und in
die Innenhöfe und eine abwechslungsrei-
che Lichtführung charakterisieren das Projekt.

We presumed that the spatial requirements
of the treatment center would increase pro-
portionally with the care center. We therefore suggested a two- to three-story flat-
roof building that would facilitate fulfilling
a later need for reorganizing individual areas. We rejected the separation of care and
treatment center that was prevalent back
then. The project is characterized by the
targeted vistas that allow one to view into
the distance, and the inner courtyards and
the resulting varied light management.

P: arb mit/with Kurt Aellen, Franz Biffiger,
Urs Hettich, Daniel Reist, Bernhard Suter
A: Münsingen

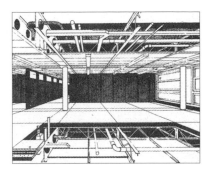

Freies Gymnasium Bern
1966 Wettbewerb/Competition
1970–72 Bau/Construction

Schulbetriebsgebäude Muri
School Building Muri
1970 Wettbewerb/Competition

Die Schulanlage liegt in einem Wohnquartier an einer stark befahrenen Strasse. Wir grenzen die Schule gegen aussen klar ab und stellen einen «Leerraum» ins Zentrum. Der Schwerpunkt dieses «Leerraumes» ist die Halle, von der aus alle Raumgruppen – Klassenzimmer, Aula, Verwaltung, Turnhalle, Werkräume, Sprachlabor und Abwartwohnung – und auch die Pausenplätze und der Biologiegarten im Freien erschlossen werden. Eine Aluminium-Vorhangfassade umschliesst die ganze Anlage.

The grammar school complex is located in a housing quarter on a street with heavy traffic. We clearly demarcated the school from the outside and placed an "empty space" in the center. The focal point of this "empty space" is the hall, from which all groups of rooms – classrooms, foyer, administration, gymnasium, workshops, language laboratory and caretaker's apartment – as well as the schoolyards and the biology garden outside can be accessed. An aluminum curtain façade surrounds the entire complex.

P: Daniel Reist, R: arb, A: Beaulieustrasse 56, Bern

Weil sich Ausbildungsmethoden wandeln, leiten wir die Raumform nicht aus den momentanen Anforderungen ab. Wir schlagen einen Grossraum vor, der so weit als möglich frei organisiert und genutzt werden kann. Die Anlage ermöglicht räumliche Kontinuität, freie Beleuchtung und eine einfache Baustruktur. Aufgrund der Vorschriften über Abstände von Gebäuden benötigt die kompakte eingeschossige Halle nicht mehr Landfläche als mehrgeschossige Anlagen und ist dank der gewählten Baustruktur wirtschaftlich.

Because education methods change, we didn't derive the spatial form from the existing requirements. We suggested a large room that can be organized and used as freely as possible. The layout allows for spatial continuity, free lighting and a simple building structure. Given the regulations concerning the distance between buildings, the compact one-story hall doesn't require more land than multi-story complexes, and, thanks to the chosen building structure, it is economically efficient.

P: arb mit/with Kurt Aellen, Franz Biffiger, Urs Hettich, Daniel Reist, Bernhard Suter, A: Moosstrasse, Muri bei Bern

ANHANG
APPENDIX

Entstehung und Struktur von arb

Kurt Aellen, Franz Biffiger, Urs Hettich, Daniel Reist und Bernhard Suter gründen 1968 als vorerst lockerer Zusammenschluss von Einzelbüros die arb Arbeitsgruppe. Ziel ist der Auftritt als Team im Hinblick auf die Steigerung der Leistungsfähigkeit, ohne dabei die Autonomie der Einzelbüros völlig aufzugeben. Urs Hettich wird 1972 Kantonsbaumeister des Kantons Bern, 1975 trennt sich Bernhard Suter von arb, 1978 wird Daniel Reist Stadtplaner in Bern. 1980 treten Peter Keller und Thomas Keller als neue Partner ein. Die Führung der arb Arbeitsgruppe erfolgt nun kollektiv durch diese vier Partner. Horizontal organisierte Projektgruppen begleiten die Projekte unter der Leitung eines Partners durch alle Phasen. Die Projektgruppen werden entsprechend den Aufgaben immer wieder neu zusammengestellt.

Die vier Partner von arb

Kurt Aellen, geboren 1938. Von 1958–66 Architekturstudium in Lausanne, Diplom 1966 bei Prof. Hans Brechbühler. Assistent bei Brechbühler und Mitarbeiter in dessen Büros in Lausanne und Bern, Metallbau und Fassadenstudien in Zusammenarbeit mit Jean Prouvé. Mitbegründer der arb Arbeitsgruppe 1968. 1970–73 Arbeit als freier Mitarbeiter an Infrastrukturprojekten in Algerien. 1976 Gastdozent an der EPFL in Lausanne. Seit 1995 Gastdozent am Institut d'Architecture de l'Université de Genève. Mitgliedschaften: SIA (Präsident seit 1996), BSA (Mitglied Zentralvorstand 1978–84), SWB, REG (Mitglied der Prüfungskommission), 1980–88 Kantonale Kunstkommission (Präsident).

Franz Biffiger, geboren 1939. Von 1960–65 Architekturstudium in Zürich, Diplom 1965/66 bei Prof. Paul Waltenspühl. Vor und nach dem Diplom Mitarbeit im Atelier 5. 1967/68 Studienarbeiten für IGECO. 1968 Mitbegründer der arb Arbeitsgruppe. Mitgliedschaften: SIA, BSA, SWB. Langjähriger Prä-

Evolution and Structure of arb

Kurt Aellen, Franz Biffiger, Urs Hettich, Daniel Reist and Berhard Suter founded the arb work group in 1968, at first, as a loose merger between individual offices. The goal was the joint presentation as a team with respect to increasing performance without completely abandoning the autonomy of the individual offices. Urs Hettich became the offical architect for the Canton of Bern in 1972, and in 1975 Bernhard Suter left arb. In 1978, Daniel Reist became an urban planner in Bern. In 1980, Peter and Thomas Keller joined as new partners. The arb work group is now managed collectively by these four partners. Project groups with a horizontal organization accompany the projects under the management of one of the partners through all phases. The project groups are formed according to the tasks for each project.

The Four Partners at arb

Kurt Aellen, born 1938. From 1958–66 he studied architecture in Lausanne, diploma work in 1966 with Prof. Hans Brechbühler. Assistant with Prof. Hans Brechbühler and co-worker in his offices in Lausanne and Bern. Metal construction and façade studies in collaboration with Jean Prouvé. Co-founder of the arb work group in 1968. 1970–73 he worked as a freelancer on infrastructure projects in Algeria. 1976 guest lecturer at EPFL in Lausanne. Since 1995, guest lecturer at the Institut d'Architecture de l'Université de Genève. Memberships: SIA (President since 1996), BSA (central board member 1978–84), SWB, REG (member of the board of examiners), 1980–88 Cantonal Art Commission (President).

Franz Biffiger, born 1939. From 1960–65 he studied architecture in Zurich, diploma work in 1965/66 with Prof. Paul Waltenspühl. Before and after receiving his degree, collaboration in Atelier 5. In 1967/68 studies for IGECO. 1968 co-founder of arb work group. Memberships: SIA, BSA, SWB,

sident des BFP (Berner Fachausschuss für Planungsfragen). 1972–77 Mitglied des Stadtparlaments, 1976–93 des Kantonsparlaments. Aktiver Jazzpianist, seit 1984 Präsident der Swiss Jazz School.

Peter Keller, geboren 1937. Von 1957–59 Architekturstudium in Zürich, 1960–64 in Lausanne, Diplom 1964/65 bei Prof. Pierre Foretay. Mitarbeit im Stadtplanungsamt Bern von 1965–66. In New York 1966–68 in verschiedenen Büros tätig. Von 1968–74 Bauinspektor/Bauverwalter der Gemeinde Muri bei Bern. 1974–75 Stadtplaner in Biel. Ab 1975 bei der arb Arbeitsgruppe, 1976–78 Coopérant technique in Algerien, Partner seit 1980. Mitgliedschaften: SIA, SWB.

Thomas Keller, geboren 1940. Von 1962–67 Architekturstudium in Zürich und Projektjahr bei Prof. Julian Beinart in Cape Town, Diplom 1967/68 bei Prof. Alfred Roth, anschliessend im ORL-Institut Mitarbeit an den landesplanerischen Leitbildern für die Schweiz. 1969–71 im Büro von Eva und Nils Koppel in Kopenhagen. 1972 Aufenthalt in Afrika. 1973–79 bei Planconsult in Basel. Ab 1979 bei der arb Arbeitsgruppe, Partner seit 1980. Mitgliedschaft: SIA

Bern Expert Committee for Planning (President for many years). 1972–77 member of the city parliament, 1976–93 member of the cantonal parliament. Active jazz pianist, since 1984 President of the Swiss Jazz School.

Peter Keller, born 1937. From 1957–59 he studied architecture in Zurich, 1960–64 in Lausanne. Diploma in 1964/65 with Prof. Pierre Foretay. Collaboration in the Bern urban planning administration from 1965–66. He worked in various offices in New York from 1966-68. From 1968–74 building inspector/administrator for the community of Muri near Bern. 1974–75 urban planner in Biel. He has been with the arb work group since 1975, 1976–78 Coopérant technique in Algeria, a partner since 1980. Memberships: SIA, SWB.

Thomas Keller, born 1940. From 1962–67 he studied architecture in Zurich and spent a project year with Prof. Julian Beinart in Cape Town. Diploma work in 1967/68 with Prof. Alfred Roth, and afterwards, collaboration at the ORL Institute on the national planning models for Switzerland. 1969–71 in the office of Eva and Nils Koppel in Copenhagen. 1972 he was back in Africa. 1973–79 with Planconsult in Basel. He joined the arb work group in 1979 and has been a partner since 1980. Membership: SIA.

ARB ARBEITSGEMEINSCHAFT (1980–1999)

Katrin Aellen, Lehrtochter; Kurt Aellen, Architekt EPFL; Tom Aellen, Modellbau; Fredua Agyemang, Praktikant aus Ghana; Nicole Almia-Jacot, Lehrtochter/Hochbauzeichnerin; Victor Alther, Bauführer; Kobi Atias, Praktikant Technion-Israel Institute of Technology; Hansruedi Bader, Praktikant HTL; Nouha Baghdadi, Praktikantin EPFL; Cédric Bart, Praktikant EPFL; Fritz Baumann, Hochbauzeichner; Helen Becket, Praktikantin University of Liverpool; Franz Biffiger, Architekt ETHZ; Regina Biffiger, Lehrtochter/Hochbauzeichnerin; Michael Bigler, Lehrling; Franziska Binggeli, Sekretärin; Simon Bode, Praktikant University of Liverpool; Hanspeter Bürgi, Architekt ETHZ; Laurent Cantalou, Architekt EPFL; Regina Christinat Balsiger, Sekretärin; Melecio Colonia, Lehrling; Craig Deane, Praktikant University of Liverpool; Kathrin Eichenberger-Thomann, Innenarchitektin (freie Mitarbeiterin); Natalie Fahrni, Sekretärin; Jonathan Falkingham, Praktikant University of Liverpool; Beatrice Finger, Sekretärin; Adam Firth, Praktikant University of Liverpool; Thomas Flückiger, Lehrling; Rudenz Flühmann, Lehrling/Student/Architekt HTL; Ian Keith Ford, Praktikant University of Liverpool; Christoph Frautschi, Architekt ETHZ; Beatrice Friedli, Lehrtochter; Ariana Furlan, Praktikantin Universität Ljubljana; Ronald Gall, Hochbauzeichner; Philippe Genoux, Student HTL; Caroline Genoux-Batsalle, Architektin Ecole d'Architecture de Marseille; Christine Gosteli, Hochbauzeichnerin; Nicole Götti, Lehrtochter; Jürg Grunder, Architekt HTL; Peter Grueneisen, Architekt HTL; Michael Hodel, Lehrling; Vesa Honkonen, Praktikant TU Helsinki; Urs Huber, Architekt HTL; Renata Hubschmied, Sekretärin; Mountassir Ilyassa, Architekt Ecole d'Architecture de Marseille; Ivan Itschner, Praktikant ETHZ; Valérie Jaccottet, Architektin EPFL; Christophe Jeanprêtre, Architekt EPFL; Andrea Jenzer, Lehrtochter; Elisabeth Jordi, Hochbauzeichnerin; Kurt Jutzi, Lehrling; Elisabeth Kappeler, Hochbauzeichnerin; Peter Keller, Architekt EPFL; Thomas Keller, Architekt ETHZ; Alain Krähenbühl, Bauführer; Joanne Krebs-Wells, Praktikantin University of Liverpool/Architektin; Jens Langsch, Bauführer; Anke Lifka, Praktikantin Universität Kaiserslautern; Danielle Liniger, Lehrtochter; Rebecca Lyon Stanton, Architektin EPFL; Silvia Mainberger, Praktikantin ETHZ; Alexander Morris, Praktikant University of Liverpool; Beatrice Mollet, Sekretärin; Alain Mosimann, Lehrling/Hochbauzeichner; Eliane Müller, Hochbauzeichnerin; Christine Odermatt-Burri, Architektin ETHZ; Claire Oxley, Praktikantin University of Liverpool; Beatrice Pahud, Sekretärin; Mauro Pompizi, Student/Architekt HTL; Kathrin Preiswerk, Lehrtochter; Reto Prina, Praktikant ETHZ; Joanne-Claire Puller, Praktikantin University of Liverpool; Pascal Pythoud, Architekt HTL; Vinzenz Reist, Praktikant ETHZ; Mario Ricklin, Architekt HTL; Gareth Roberts, Praktikant University of Liverpool; Peter Rothenbühler, Hochbauzeichner; Hans Ruchti, Bauführer; Alvaro Sahonero, Praktikant, Bolivien; Marcello Sartorio, Bauführer; Gerhard Schläfli, Bauführer; Susanne Seiler, Praktikantin HTL; Ian Shaw, Praktikant University of Liverpool; Patrick Sheridan, Praktikant University of Liverpool; Boris Siebold, Praktikant IAUG; Harald Siegrist, Lehrling; Ruedi Spring, Architekt HTL; Hans Stäubli, Architekt HTL; Daniel Steck, Architekt ETHZ; Franziska Steinmann, Lehrtochter; John Stephenson, Dozent University of Liverpool; Thomas Steuri, Praktikant/Werklehrer; Alex Szankasy, Architekt IAUG; Manuel Vatter, Praktikant ETHZ; Gisela Vollmer, Architektin TU Dresden; Rolf von Allmen, Architekt HTL; Chantal Weidmann, Architektin EPFL; Bruno Wermuth, Student/Architekt HTL; Adrian Wiesmann, Student HTL; Markus Wyss, Student/Architekt HTL; Martin Wyss, Architekt ETHZ; Urs Zemp, Student/Architekt HTL; Christine Zimmermann, Hochbauzeichnerin; Martin Zürcher, Architekt ETHZ

Bis in die achtziger Jahre beschränkten sich in Liverpool unsere Kenntnisse der Schweiz auf die Naturschönheiten, ihre Neutralität, ihre Lage in der Europäischen Mitte, sowie auf die Schriften von Kidder Smith über die fünfziger Jahre, Rossi's Beiträge der siebziger und die Arbeiten der «Tessiner Schule» in den achtzigern.

Zufällig ergab sich 1984 für einen unserer Studenten die Möglichkeit, sein einjähriges Praktikum innerhalb des sechsjährigen Studiums bei arb zu absolvieren. Damit begann eine 15 Jahre andauernde, bereichernde und fruchtbare Beziehung zwischen arb und den Studenten und Studentinnen und besonders auch John Stephenson, Dozent an der Architekturschule der Universität Liverpool, der ältesten und womöglich bekanntesten in Grossbritannien. Zu jener Zeit war die Architektur Grossbritanniens durch die fragwürdigen Strömungen der Postmoderne aus den USA beeinflusst. Der neue Bezug zu arb machte bald klar, dass die anderswo aufgegebenen Werte einer zeitgemässen «Moderne» in der Schweiz, in Finnland und möglicherweise auch in Holland weiter gepflegt werden. Erfrischende Werte, die in Bauten aller Schweizer Kantone erkennbar waren, selbst im eigenständigen Tessin. Uns manifestierte sich fast überall gute bauliche und handwerkliche Qualität. Die menschlichen Grundwerte sahen wir respektiert. Wir erkannten dieselbe Strenge und Klarheit, welche viele unserer Gebäude aus der Zeit der industriellen Revolution des 19. Jahrhunderts kennzeichnen, speziell im Norden Englands. In Manchester und Liverpool sind manche dieser Bauten Beispiele eleganter Ingenieurkunst, verfeinert mit architektonischem Gespür. In Liverpool kommen diese Tugenden am besten in den Dockanlagen zum Ausdruck, speziell im «Albert Dock» von Jesse Hartley. In «The Functional Tradition» zeigt J.M. Richards diese Werte, welche jetzt gewisse britische Architekten mit spektakulärem Erfolg in England und Übersee, besonders im Pazifischen Raum, wiederentdecken.

Until the 1980's our knowledge in Liverpool of Switzerland and the Swiss was limited to the natural qualities arising from its location, neutrality, and European centrality together with the writings of Kidder Smith on the 50's, Rossi in the 70's and the works of the Tessin architects in the 80's.

By chance, in 1984 the opportunity arose from IAESTE (International Association for the Exchange of Students for Technical Experience) for one of our students to spend a "Year in Practice", in the middle of our 6 year course, with arb Arbeitsgruppe. Thus began a 15-year, continually rich and rewarding relationship between arb, Liverpool University School of Architecture, the oldest and arguably the best known U.K. Schools, our students, and, not least, John Stephenson, one of their tutors.

At that time, architecture in the UK was beeing influenced by the USA by the false values of post modernism. The new relationship with arb quickly demonstrated that the discarded values of a contemporary modernism were alive and well in Switzerland, as well as in Finland and possibly Holland. These values were refreshingly clear in the general architecture of all Cantons, even in the idiosynchratic Tessin. To our eyes and minds it was almost all of high quality, respecting basic human values, and always very well crafted. It had similar qualities of toughness and clarity which characterised many of our buildings of the 19th. century industrial revolution, particularly in northern England. Many of these in Manchester and Liverpool are fine examples of elegant engineering coupled with refined architectural sensibilties. Liverpool's best are the docks, especially the Albert Dock by Jesse Hartley.

J.M. Richards, in "The Functional Tradition", clearly identifies these qualities and they are now being rediscovered by many UK architects with spectacular results both at home and overseas, particularly the Pacific Rim.

arb Arbeitsgruppe crystallise these values in their own manner, embodying architec-

arb kristallisiert diese Werte auf ihre eigene Weise, indem sie architektonische Qualität, soziale Verantwortung und handwerkliche Perfektion des Details verbinden. Was mehr kann sich ein Praktikant als Einführung in das Handwerk des Häusermachens wünschen? Eine geistesverwandte Atmosphäre, warmherzige Menschen mit Stärken aber auch Schwächen und Fehlern.
Weder unsere 13 Studenten noch ihr Betreuer, die bei arb gearbeitet haben, wurden je enttäuscht. Alle schätzten die Gruppe, die sich höchsten qualitativen Anforderungen verpflichtet, keine Anstrengung scheut, wenn nötig durcharbeitet und dies alles in den Räumen einer «elektronischen Scheune». Diese kontrastiert heute mit dem benachbarten «Haus Brunnadern» in dem auch einige arb-Mitarbeiter wohnen. Vielleicht versinnbildlichen diese zwei Gebäude die Entwicklung von arb der letzten 30 Jahre.

Gut dass die Beziehungen auch in umgekehrter Richtung funktionieren. 1997 haben Thomas Keller und Kurt Aellen Liverpool besucht, um an unserer Universität vor «vollem Haus» von Studenten und Lehrern einen Vortrag zu halten. Noch heute, zwei Jahre danach, erinnern wir uns mit grosser Freude daran.
Unser erster Praktikant bei arb 1984, Jonathan Falkingham, nun selbst erfolgreich praktizierender Architekt, konnte Kurt und Thomas seine eigenen Werke und Liverpools beste Dockanlagen zeigen. Die Qualitätsvorstellungen aller drei Architekten stimmten überein, sie lassen sich so umschreiben: «Architektur von hoher Qualität als eine soziale Kunst mit sozialen Mitteln für einen sozialen Zweck».
Freundschaft, basierend auf gemeinschaftlichen Bestrebungen hält die Welt in Gang. Wir in Liverpool schätzen das. Lang möge es dauern. Mit freundlichen Grüssen aus dem nicht so fernen Norden

John Stephenson, Jack Dunne
und die Studenten der School of Architecture, University of Liverpool

tonic qualities, social sensibilities and a devotion to crafting down to the smallest detail. What more could a young "Year in Practice" student wish for as an introduction to the practice of making buildings? He or she might wish for a congenial atmosphere peopled by warm human beings, mostly with strengths but also with human failings.
None of our 13 students or their tutor who have worked at arb were disappointed. All appreciated the totality of warm personalities dedicated to the highest quality design, working all hours, playing hard, and valuing every endeavour, all in the physical setting of an "Electronic Barn". The "Electronic Barn" now contrasts with the adjacent "House Brunnadern" housing, amongst other users, many of the arb co-workers. Perhaps these two buildings epitomise the progress of arb over the past 30 years and a portent for the future.

It is good that the relationship also works in the opposite geographical direction.
In 1997 Thomas Keller and Kurt Aellen visited Liverpool to give a presentation to a "Full House" of students and staff at our University. It is still remembered with great pleasure 2 years later.
Our first student at arb in 1984, Jonathan Falkingham, now successfully in his own entrepreneurial practice, was able to give Kurt and Thomas a tour of his own designed works and a tour of Liverpool's best dock buildings. The connection in quality between all 3 architectures was clear and pleasing and reflecting "Architecture of high quality as a social art by social means for a social purpose".
Friendship based on a common endeavour is what makes part of the world go round. We in Liverpool value that. Long may it continue. With love and respect from the not-so-far-north

John Stephenson, Jack Dunne
and the students of the School of Architecture, University of Liverpool

Lore Ditzen

Berlinerin aus ehemals deutschen östlichen Grenzgebieten, studierte Kunstgeschichte und Literatur. Im Hauptberuf war sie für etliche Dezennien als Kultur-Redakteurin beim Sender Freies Berlin tätig. Dort machte sie – angeregt durch die «Wohnungsnutzungsuntersuchung» im internationalen Berliner Hansaviertel von 1957 – Bauen, Wohnen und Stadterhaltung zu einem ständigen Thema, über das sie auch in Zeitungen und Zeitschriften schrieb. 1975 erhielt sie den Journalistenpreis des Deutschen Nationalkomitees für Denkmalschutz. Acht Jahre lang gehörte sie, als Mitglied des Deutschen Werkbundes Berlin, zur Redaktionsgruppe von «Werk und Zeit». Im Zusammenhang mit dieser Arbeit entstanden auch Fernsehfilme über den Sozialen Wohnungsbau und über Bruno Tauts «Onkel Toms Hütte». Ihrem Beruf verdankt sie «die Begegnung mit wunderbaren Menschen und lebenslanges Lernen».

Peter Grueneisen

Geboren 1960, lebt in Los Angeles. Architekt AIA (American Institute of Architects). Ausbildung: 1980 Hochbauzeichner; 1983 Architekt HTL; 1990 Master of Architecture, Southern California Institute of Architecture (SCI-Arc), Santa Monica. Arbeit: 1983–1987 Projektarchitekt und Bauleitung bei «arb Arbeitsgruppe» in Bern»; 1987–1988 Projektentwerfer bei «Glaser & Associates» in Cincinnati, Ohio; 1983–1989 Inhaber «ParaDOX Design»; 1990 Gründer und seither Entwurfspartner bei Studio «bau:ton», Los Angeles. Auszeichnungen: 1992 Honor Award und 1994 Merit Award der AIA/Los Angeles; 1994 Gewinner TEC-Award für aussergewöhnliche Leistungen in Akustik und Studio-Design.

Arthur Kirchhofer

Geboren 1953, lebt in Gümmenen, BE. Studium der Biologie an der Universität Bern (1978–1984), Promotion über Limnologie und Fischbiologie (1990), Oberassistent an der Universität Bern (bis 1996). Seit 1996

Lore Ditzen

From Berlin and the former East German border area, Ditzen studied art history and literature. In her primary career, she worked as a cultural editor with the radio station Freies Berlin for several decades. Inspired by the "apartment utilization inquiry" in the international Berlin Hansa quarter from 1957, she made architecture, living and urban preservation a permanent theme there and also wrote about it in newspapers and magazines. In 1975 she received a journalistic award from the German National Committee for Historic Monuments. For eight years she was in the editor's group of "Werk und Zeit" as a member of the Deutsche Werkbund Berlin. In connection with this work, TV films about social housing and Bruno Taut's "Uncle Tom's Cabin" were created. She owes her profession to "the encounter with wonderful people and life-long learning."

Peter Grueneisen

Born in 1960, Grueneisen lives in Los Angeles. Architect AIA (American Institute of Architects). Training: 1980 structural engineering draftsman; 1983 architect HTL; 1990 Master of Architecture, Southern California Institute of Architecture, (SCI-Arc) Santa Monica. Work: 1983–1987 project architect and building supervisor with "arb Arbeitsgruppe in Bern;" 1987–1988 project designer with "Glaser & Associates" in Cincinnati, Ohio; 1983–1989 owner "ParaDOX Design"; 1990 founder and since then design partner with studio "bau:ton", Los Angeles. Awards: 1992 Honor Award and 1994 Merit Award of AIA/Los Angeles; 1994 winner TEC-Award for unusual achievements in acoustic and studio design.

Arthur Kirchhofer

Born in 1953, Kirchhofer lives in Gümmenen, BE. He studied biology at Bern University (1978–1984), doctorate in limnology and marine biology (1990), head assistant at Bern University (until 1996). Since 1996 he has been the owner of an environ-

Inhaber eines Umweltberatungsbüros für die Spezialgebiete Gewässerökologie, Fischbiologie und Naturschutz (GFN).

Therese Lindt Kirchhofer
Geboren 1953, lebt in Gümmenen, BE. Studium der Biologie an der Universität Bern (1978–1983), Promotion über Pflanzenphysiologie (1987), verschiedene Arbeiten auf den Gebieten Umwelttoxikologie und -analytik. Seit 1997 Mitarbeiterin im Büro GFN.

Benedikt Loderer
1945 in Bern geboren, studierte nach einer Bauzeichnerlehre und der Matura auf dem zweiten Bildungsweg Architektur an der ETH Zürich. Anschliessend war er Hochschulassistent, Fernsehvolontär und angestellter Architekt. Dann driftete er ins Zeitungsschreiben ab und war einige Jahre freier Journalist, namentlich als «Stadtwanderer» und Architekturkritiker beim Zürcher «Tages-Anzeiger». «Der Innenraum des Aussenraums ist Aussenraum des Innenraums» war der Titel seiner Dissertation, die er 1981 abschloss. Zwischen 1980 und 1986 schrieb er drei Hörspiele und ein Fernsehstück und war Teilzeitredaktor der Architekturzeitschrift «aktuelles bauen». Im Verlag Curti Medien AG gab er 1988 den Anstoss zur Gründung der Illustrierten für Gestaltung und Architektur «Hochparterre», deren Chefredaktor er wurde. Im Sommer 1991 wurde aus «Hochparterre» ein redaktionseigener Betrieb, die Zeitschrift gehört seither ihren Machern. Im Mai 1997 trat er als Chefredaktor zurück und wurde Redaktor und Stadtwanderer ohne Führungsaufgabe bei «Hochparterre». Loderer kann drei Dinge: Lesen, schreiben, reden.

Peter Lüem
Geboren 1958, lebt in Zürich. Ausbildung: Matur; Mimenschule Lecoq, Paris; Fotofachklasse der Schule für Gestaltung, Zürich. Arbeitet seit 1989 als selbständiger Fotograf in den Bereichen Architektur, Landschaftsdokumentation und Illustration, sowie als Künstler (Fotografie, Installationen, Videos).

mental consultation office for the fields of water ecology, marine biology and conservation (GFN).

Therese Lindt Kirchhofer
Born in 1953, Therese Lindt Kirchhofer lives in Gümmenen, BE. She studied biology at Bern University (1978–1983), doctorate in plant physiology (1987), various work in the fields of environmental toxicology and analysis. Since 1997 collaborator in the office GFN.

Benedikt Loderer
Born in Bern in 1945, Loderer studied architecture at ETH Zurich after his training as a construction draftsman and his final exams. Following his studies, he was a university assistant, an unpaid TV trainee and employed architect. He then drifted into writing for newspapers and was a freelance journalist for several years, namely as the "urban wanderer" and architectural critic with the Zurich "Tages-Anzeiger." The title of his dissertation, which he finished in 1981, was "The interior of the exterior is the exterior of the interior." Between 1980 and 1986 he wrote three radio plays and a TV play and was a part-time editor of the architectural magazine "aktuelles bauen." With Curti Medien AG publishers he initiated the foundation of the magazine "Hochparterre" in 1988, and became editor-in-chief. In summer 1991 "Hochparterre" became an editor-owned enterprise; the magazine has since then been owned by its makers. In May 1997 he resigned as editor-in-chief and became editor and urban wanderer without executive task with "Hochparterre." Loderer knows to do three things: read, write, speak.

Peter Lüem
Born in 1958, Lüem lives in Zurich. Training: final exam; mime school Lecoq, Paris; photography class at the Zurich Design School. Has been working as a self-employed photographer since 1989 in the fields of architecture, landscape documentation and illustration an as an artist (photography, installations, videos).

John Stephenson
Architekt, Städteplaner und Dozent. Geboren 1930. Promovierte an der Universität von Manchester 6 Jahre vor Norman Foster. Ehemals Städteplaner bei «Warrington», einer britischen Firma für Städteneubau. 19 Jahre lang Partner der «Design Group Partnership» in Chester, England, spezialisiert für sozialen Wohnungsbau, Schulen und Spitäler. «Year Master», Design-Lehrer und Dozent an der Universität von Liverpool während 20 Jahren. Hat ein spezielles Interesse am «Ökologischen Bauen» und an den Pueblos des 12. Jahrhunderts, der Architektur der Ureinwohner. Sehr geschätzt hat er die 16jährige Beziehung und Freundschaft zu arb als Mitarbeiter und als Betreuer von Studenten.

Dominique Uldry
1953 in Lausanne geboren, aufgewachsen in Bern. Autodidakt. Seit 1983 freischaffend. 1982 und 1988 Eidgenössische Stipendien für angewandte Kunst; 1987 Stipendiat an der Cité des Arts in Paris; Arbeitet hauptsächlich auf den Gebieten der Architekturfotografie und der Kunstdokumentation. Teilnahme an diversen Ausstellungen, u.a.: 1984 Abbruchgalerie Bern; 1988 Kunst mit Fotografie, Kunstmuseum Bern; 1996 Kunstkanal Bern; 1998 Fotorelations, Kunsthaus Brünn, Kunstraum Burgdorf.

John Stephenson
Architect, Urban Planner and Lecturer. Born 1930. Graduated from Manchester University 6 years before Norman Foster. Sometime Urban Planner at "Warrington" New Town Development Corporation, U.K. Partner "Design Group Partnership" Chester, U.K. for 19 years, specialising in social housing, schools and hospitals. Year Master, Design Tutor and Lecturer at the University of Liverpool for 20 years. Special interests are in ecological architecture and the architecture of the 12th century pueblo native Americans. Most valued has been the 16-year relationship and friendship as a worker and student tutor with arb Arbeitsgruppe, Bern.

Dominique Uldry
Was born 1953 in Lausanne and grew up in Bern. Autodidactic. Since 1983 free-lance work. 1982 and 1988 Swiss scholarships for applied arts; 1987 sholarship at Cité des Arts in Paris; mainly works in the fields of architectural photography and art documentation. Participation in various exhibitions, among them: 1984 Abbruchgalerie Bern; 1988 Kunst mit Fotografie, Kunstmuseum Bern; 1996 Kunstkanal Bern; 1998 Fotorelations, Kunsthaus Brünn, Kunstraum Burgdorf.

BAUINGENIEURE
CIVIC ENGINEERS

Arnold AG, Kaufdorf
Anbau Haus Messerli, Addition House
Messerli
Bächtold AG, Bern
Schanzenpost
SRG und SRI, SRG and SRI;
Emch + Berger AG, Bern
Paketverarbeitungszentren, Package
Handling Centers; Schanzenpost;
Umbau Nationalbank Bern,
Conversion Nationalbank Bern;
Verwaltungsgebäude City West,
Administrative Building City West;
Wohnbauten Stiglenstrasse,
Apartment Buildings Stiglenstrasse;
Wohnbauten Vermontpark, Apartment
Buildings Vermont Park
Hartenbach + Wenger AG, Bern
Fernmeldedirektion Bern,
Telecommunications Direction Bern;
Schanzenpost
Kappeler, Gümligen
Kindergarten Seidenberg
Lüthy M., Bern
Schanzenpost
Marchand G., Bern
Freies Gymnasium Bern, Grammar
School Bern
Mange + Müller AG, Bern
Fernmeldedirektion Bern,
Telecommunications Direction Bern;
Mattesteg
Moor + Hauser AG, Bern
BFF-Schule Bern, BFF School Bern;
Pachtgut Bannholz, Lease Farm
Bannholz
Moser A., Zumikon
Turm auf dem Ulmizberg, Tower on
Ulmizberg
Naef + Partner, Bern
Masterplan Bahnhof Bern, Master
Plan Bern Station
Niederhäuser P.A., Bévilard
Behindertenheim La Pimpinière, Home
for the Handicapped La Pimpinière
Sahli R., Bern
Oberes Murifeld

Schlup + Zanetti, Langenthal
Sanitätspolizei
Schneller Rytz und Partner, Brig
Centre Radio-Télévision Sion 2006;
Paketverarbeitungszentren, Package
Handling Centers
Stocker H.P. + Partner AG, Bern
Schulheim Schloss Erlach, School
Hostel Erlach Castle; Schul-und
Kirchgemeindezentrum Neuenegg,
School and Church Community Center
Neuenegg; Siedlung Hintere Aumatt,
Development Hintere Aumatt; Sied-
lung Merzenacker, Development
Merzenacker; Städtische Reitschule,
Municipal Riding-School; Turm auf
dem Ulmizberg, Tower on Ulmizberg
SMT + Partner, Bern
Atriumhäuser Kalchacker, Atrium
Houses Kalchacker; Haus Brunnadern,
House Brunnadern; Verwaltungsge-
bäude Valiant Holding, Administrative
Headquartes Valiant Holding
Studer, Mauch, Kohler, Bern
BFF-Schule Bern, BFF School Bern
Theiler Ingenieure AG, Thun
Schweizer Armeemuseum,
Swiss Army Museum
Zimmermann + Tellenbach SA, Tavannes
Behindertenheim La Pimpinière, Home
for the Handicapped La Pimpinière

SPEZIAL-INGENIEURE/FACHPLANER
SPECIAL ENGINEERS/EXPERT PLANNERS

Amstein + Walthert, Bern/Zürich
Verwaltungsgebäude City West,
Administrative Building City West;
Verwaltungsgebäude Valiant Holding,
Administrative Headquartes Valiant
Holding; Wohnbauten Stiglenstrasse,
Apartment Buildings Stiglenstrasse
Arm E., Bern
Oberes Murifeld
Autophon, Bern
Sanitätspolizei
Bakoplan AG, Ittigen
Schanzenpost
Bauer F. AG, Bern
BFF-Schule Bern, BFF School Bern

Baumann HT AG, Bern
  Turm auf dem Ulmizberg, Tower on
  Ulmizberg
Bering AG, Bern
  BFF-Schule Bern, BFF School Bern;
  Umbau Nationalbank Bern, Conver-
  sion Nationalbank Bern
BKW FMB Energie AG, Bern
  Schulheim Schloss Erlach, School
  Hostel Erlach Castle; Siedlung
  Hintere Aumatt, Development Hintere
  Aumatt
Boess+Partner AG, Bern
  Fernmeldedirektion Bern, Telecom-
  munications Direction Bern
Brücker Ingenieure AG, Muri b. Bern
  Oberes Murifeld; Siedlung Hintere
  Aumatt, Development Hintere Aumatt
Bucknell, Austin and Partner, London
  Mufindi Township
Chapuis+Zürcher AG, Bern
  Wohnbauten Vermontpark, Apartment
  Buildings Vermont Park
CSD Colombi Schmutz Dorthe AG, Bern
  und Sion
  Centre Radio-Télévision Sion 2006;
  Paketverarbeitungszentren, Package
  Handling Centers
Eicher Dr.+Pauli AG, Bern
  Siedlung Hintere Aumatt, Develop-
  ment Hintere Aumatt
Elektro Hardy Walther AG, Bern
  Haus Brunnadern, House Brunnadern
Enerconom AG, Bern
  Städtische Reitschule, Municipal
  Riding-School
ETE, Lausanne
  Schul- und Kirchgemeindezentrum
  Neuenegg, School and Church
  Community Center
EWB, Bern
  BFF-Schule Bern, BFF School Bern;
  Sanitätspolizei
EWE, Bern
  Schanzenpost
Fasel + Brunner, Bern
  Haus Brunnadern, House Brunnadern
Friedli, Muri b. Bern
  Wohnbauten Vermontpark, Apartment
  Buildings Vermont Park

Gartenmann Engineering AG, Bern
  Siedlung Hintere Aumatt;
  Development Hintere Aumatt
Gerber Rolf AG, Bern
  Atriumhäuser Kalchacker, Atrium
  Houses Kalchacker
Griner, Bern
  Freies Gymnasium Bern
Grize AG, Muri b. Bern
  Atriumhäuser Kalchacker, Atrium
  Houses Kalchacker
Grolimund + Partner AG, Bern
  Haus Brunnadern, House Brunnadern;
  Schanzenpost; Schweizer
  Armeemuseum, Swiss Army Museum;
  SRG und SRI, SRG and SRI; Städtische
  Reitschule, Municipal Riding-School;
  Verwaltungsgebäude Valiant Holding,
  Administrative Headquartes Valiant
  Holding; Wohnbauten Stiglenstrasse,
  Apartment Buildings Stiglenstrasse;
  Atriumhäuser Kalchacker, Atrium
  Houses Kalchacker
Gruner AG, Basel
  Industriegebiet Abuja, Industrial Area
  Abuja
Gwerder, Bern
  Städtische Reitschule, Municipal
  Riding-School
Hämmann, Hinterkappelen
  Fernmeldedirektion Bern,
  Telecommunications Direction Bern;
  Siedlung Hintere Aumatt, Develop-
  ment Hintere Aumatt
H + S Technik AG, Thun
  Schweizer Armeemuseum, Swiss Army
  Museum
Imbaumgarten Ing.Büro, Bern
  Verwaltungsgebäude City West,
  Administrative Building City West;
  Wohnbauten Stiglenstrasse,
  Apartment Buildings Stiglenstrasse
Kalt AG, Gümligen
  Verwaltungsgebäude Valiant Holding,
  Administrative Headquartes Valiant
  Holding; SRG und SRI, SRG and SRI
Kissling+Zbinden AG, Bern
  Turm auf dem Ulmizberg, Tower on
  Ulmizberg
Linder+Lötscher, Bern
  SRG und SRI, SRG and SRI

Lutiger, Bern
Wohnbauten Vermontpark, Apartment
Buildings Vermontpark
M.G.Butech, Sonvilier
Behindertenheim La Pimpinière,
Home for the Handicapped La
Pimpinière
Messerli R. AG, Ins
Schulheim Schloss Erlach, School
Hostel Erlach Castle
Pärli, Biel
Schulheim Schloss Erlach, School
Hostel Erlach Castle
Pfister+Wyss, Wichtrach
Städtische Reitschule, Municipal
Riding-School
Rieben AG, Bern
BFF-Schule Bern, BFF School Bern
Sertech AG, Bern
Atriumhäuser Kalchacker, Atrium
Houses Kalchacker
Sifrag, Bern
Sanitätspolizei; Schulheim Schloss
Erlach, School Hostel Erlach Castle
Stadelmann Planungsbüro, Uster
Atriumhäuser Kalchacker, Atrium
Houses Kalchacker; Verwaltungsge-
bäude City West, Administrative
Building City West; Wohnbauten
Stiglenstrasse, Apartment Buildings
Stiglenstrasse
Stoffel & Co, Bern
Haus Brunnadern, House Brunnadern;
Wohnbauten Vermontpark, Apartment
Buildings Vermontpark
Strahm AG, Ittigen
Fernmeldedirektion Bern,
Telecommunications Direction Bern
Sulzer Energieconsulting AG (sec),
Gümligen
Sanitätspolizei; Schulheim Schloss
Erlach, School Hostel Erlach Castle;
SRG und SRI, SRG and SRI;
Verwaltungsgebäude City West,
Administrative Building City West
Swisscom, Bern
Schanzenpost; Turm auf dem
Ulmizberg, Tower on Ulmizberg;
Verwaltungsgebäude Valiant Holding,
Administrative Headquartes Valiant
Holding

Thermag SAG, Bern
Haus Brunnadern, House Brunnadern
tp AG SA / Biel
Behindertenheim La Pimpinière,
Home for the Handicapped La
Pimpinière
Varrin & Müller, Thun
Schweizer Armeemuseum, Swiss Army
Museum
Waldhauser, Münchenstein
Siedlung Hintere Aumatt,
Development Hintere Aumatt;
Siedlung Merzenacker, Development
Merzenacker
Walther, Bern
Freies Gymnasium Bern
Wanzenried+Hess, Bern
Sanitätspolizei
Wichser Ing.Büro, Zürich
SRG und SRI, SRG and SRI
Wolke P. Engineering AG, Lengnau
Schanzenpost
Zahnd, Niederwangen b. Bern
BFF-Schule Bern, BFF School Bern;
Oberes Murifeld
Zeugin Baumberatung AG, Münsingen
BFF-Schule Bern, BFF School Bern;
Wohnbauten Schönegg, Apartment
Buildings Schönegg
Ziehli + CO AG, Bern
SRG und SRI, SRG and SRI

LANDSCHAFTSARCHITEKTEN
LANDSCAPE ARCHITECTS

Borgeaud J.J., Lausanne
Paketverarbeitungszentrum Daillens,
Package Handling Center Daillens
Klötzli + Friedli, Bern
Wohnbauten Schönegg, Apartment
Buildings Schönegg; BFF-Schule
Bern, BFF School Bern
Dickmann M., Hannover
Gestaltungs- und Verkehrskonzept
Bödeli, Design and Traffic Concept
Bödeli
Rotzler S., Gockhausen
DB-Güterbahnhof Basel, Freight
Depot Basel; Verwaltungsgebäude
City West, Administrative Building

City West; Wohnbauten München
Parsing, Apartment Buildings Munich
Parsing; Wohnbauten Dellergelände
München, Apartment Buildings Deller
Grounds Munich
Vogel F., Bern
Haus Brunnadern, House Brunnadern;
Wohnbauten Freischützstrasse
München, Apartment Buildings
Freischützstrasse München
Weber + Saurer, Solothurn
Architekturschule Venedig, Archi-
tecture School Venice; Centre Radio-
Télévision Sion 2006; Mittlerer
Limmatquai Zürich

DANK

Architektur wird immer zusammen
gemacht. Zusammen mit Bauherren,
Ingenieuren, Fachplanern, den Leuten
vom Bau und in unserem Fall auch
zusammen in der Arbeitsgemeinschaft.
Allen die Projekte entwickelt haben und
sich für das Gelingen der Bauten enga-
gierten, danken wir im Namen von
arb herzlich.

Auch Bücher werden zusammen gemacht.
Wir danken allen die einen Beitrag
geliefert haben, wir danken auch allen,
die die Arbeit des Prüfens, Erwägens,
Ergänzens und Korrigierens auf sich
genommen haben.

Wir danken dem Birkhäuser Verlag für
sein Engagement. Wir danken der Stadt
Bern und dem Kanton Bern für die
finanzielle Unterstützung.

Kurt Aellen, Franz Biffiger, Peter Keller,
Thomas Keller

ACKNOWLEDGEMENTS

Architecture is always a collaborative
effort. With clients, engineers, expert
planners, the people from the construction site and, in our case, the work group.
We want to express our heartfelt thanks
in the name of arb to all of those who
have developed projects and committed
themselves to the successful outcome of
the buildings.

Books are also a cooperative effort. We
would like to thank all those who have
made contributions and also all those
who have taken on the work of proofing,
contemplating, adding and correcting.

Many thanks to Birkhäuser Publishers for
their commitment, and to the city of Bern
and the Canton Bern for their financial
support.

Kurt Aellen, Franz Biffiger, Peter Keller,
Thomas Keller

A CIP catalogue record for this book is available from the Library of Congress, Washington D.C., USA.

Die Deutsche Bibliothek - CIP-Einheitsaufnahme

ARB, Arbeitsgruppe
Kurt Aellen, Franz Biffiger, Peter Keller,
Thomas Keller <Bern>:
Arb : photos, essays, catalog /
[transl. into Engl.: Katja Steiner ;
Bruce Almberg]. - Basel ; Boston ; Berlin :
Birkhäuser, 1999
            ISBN 3-7643-6103-4 (Basel...)
            ISBN 0-8176-6103-4 (Boston)

Redaktion/Editorial: Thomas Keller,
Franz Biffiger, Marco Schibig
Übersetzung ins Englische/
Translation into English:
Katja Steiner, Bruce Almberg, Ehingen
Gestaltung/Design:
Franziska Schott & Marco Schibig, Bern
Lithos und Druck/Litho and Print:
Vögeli, Langnau
Buchbinderei/Binder:
Schuhmacher, Schmitten

© 1999 arb, Brunnadernstrasse 28b, 3006
Bern, Switzerland;
Birkhäuser – Publishers for Architecture,
P.O. Box 133, CH-4010 Basel, Switzerland.

Printed on paper produced of chlorine-free pulp. TCF∞
Printed in Switzerland
ISBN 3-7643-6103-4
ISBN 0-8176-6103-4
9 8 7 6 5 4 3 2 1